BARDOT:
Eternal Sex Goddess

BARDOT:
Eternal Sex Goddess

PETER EVANS

DRAKE PUBLISHERS INC.
NEW YORK

PUBLISHED IN 1973 BY
DRAKE PUBLISHERS, INC.
381 PARK AVENUE, SOUTH
NEW YORK, N.Y. 10016

© Peter Evans and Atticus Productions Limited, 197:

Library of Congress Cataloging in Publication
Data

Evans, Peter, 1933–
  Bardot; Eternal sex goddess

  1. Bardot, Brigitte.
PN2638.B25E9 791.43'028'0924 (B) 73-4316
ISBN 0-87749-497-5

Printed in the United States of America

Acknowledgements

I should like to express my sincere appreciation to all those people in France, Britain and the United States of America who so generously helped me with background information, anecdotes, research and personal insights. Unfortunately, it is not possible to name them all (for reasons of space, if not discretion) but I am especially grateful to:

Dirk Bogarde
Betty Box
Claudia Cardinale
Henri Clouzot
Mark Andrew Christian
John Daly
Rosine Delamare
Sacha Distel
Anne Dussart
Ghislain Dussart
Dr. Richard Gordon
Kenneth Green

Kenneth Harper
Christian Jacque
Raoul Levy (deceased)
Euan Lloyd
Johanna Morris
Francoise Pascal
Olga Horstig-Primuz
Vera Horstig-Primuz
Michael Sarne
Hal Shaper
Ralph Thomas
Roger Vadim

and, of course,
Brigitte Bardot

PHOTO CREDITS

I am grateful, too to the following photographic sources for their co-operation:

Jacket photograph: Sam Levin

Patrick Moran
Betty Box and Ralph Thomas
Peter Evans (Atticus Productions, London)
Camera Press (London)
Liverani (Rome)
P. S. Monique Valentin (Paris)
Holmes/De Raemy
Daniel Angeli (Paris)
Paul Popper
S.I.P. (Paris)
C. Martin/Dalmas
Cesar Lucas
Sam Levin
Len Sirman Press (Geneva)
S.O.D.E.P. (Paris)
Mag Bodart (Paris)
Robert Cohen, A.G.I.P.
British National Film Archive (London)
Giancarlo Dotti
Gil Lagarde
Ludo Bert (Paris)
Xavier Burgelin
Roma Press Photos
Yvon Samuel
John Fairbairn

Contents

Overture and Beginning   11

'Mama don't allow . . .'   19

Tea with Monsieur Plemianikoff   27

The Bardot Body   37

'Leading Lady Approval'   47

Smoked Salmon and Smoked Glasses   55

Eternal Damnation   63

Men Over Thirty: 'Ready for Chrysanthemums'   73

No Time to Put His Socks On . . .   87

The Dinner Circus   97

Images of Instant Mesalliance . . .   105

A Girl to 'Ignite with Sean'   113

The Dying of a Dog   121

Mister Lennon and The Maharishi Mazes   129

A Bare Removal – and a Plaster Cast   139

Index   143

Brigitte Bardot – A Filmography   149

Overture and Beginning

CHAPTER 1

IT WAS ANOTHER world then, as distant as lady wing-walkers; it was a time fixed like a desperate smile exactly midway between the Wall Street crash and the first shots of the Second World War. It was the year clowning Max Baer hammered the brave and inept Primo Carnera to the canvas a dozen times to take the heavyweight crown in the eleventh. The year Jimmy Durante first tickled the ivories with *Inka Dinka Doo*. You could buy a double bed ('hand grained, walnut enamel, coil spring and mattress complete') for less than today's price of a trattoria dinner for two. Jean Harlow, the reigning sex queen, was suing for divorce. It was the year Bonnie and Clyde were shot dead in a roadside ambush by Texas Rangers and County Sheriffs in a town called Arcadia. And John Dillinger, Public Enemy Number One, got his in Chicago. In England, letter writers to *The Times* were getting hot under the collar about the shocking 'nakedness' of hikers – hiking was the newest craze that year – who revealed their knees and sometimes even their thighs on public highways. The most popular songs were Rodgers and Hart's *Blue Moon;* Jack Teagarden's version of *Stars Fell on Alabama;* and Mae West's sly rendering of *My Old Flame*. The Nazis murdered Dollfus. Italy mobilised.

In France there were two interesting events. Only one of them was much noted at the time: Serge Stavisky, a monumental bond swindler and pimp who ran whores and crooked government officials with equal aplomb, was conveniently killed when police attempted to arrest him at his villa in Chamonix. The French Republic, emotions taut with suspicion and fury, verged on civil war: slurred and implicated politicians and bankers fought sabre duels at dawn in the Bois de Boulogne, riots erupted in towns and villages across the land, fourteen Parisians were shot dead on the Place de la Concorde. The Camille Chautemp government collapsed.

It was reasonable that small attention was paid to the other particular event in France that year. It was the birth of a six-and-a-half pound daughter to Louis and Anne-Marie Bardot on the fifth floor of 36 Avenue de la Bourdonnais in Passy, a discreetly elegant part of Paris, noted for its town houses, patisserie shops, and sleek poodles. Brigitte Bardot arrived punctually for the first and perhaps the only time in her life. It was the 28th September in the year 1934.

Like prize fighters, and some of the best courtesans, most movie stars come from the working-classes and many from harsher societies. Contrarily, Brigitte grew up amid the well-to-do comforts of conventional upper-middle-class materialism. Her privileged childhood, concurred Champs Elysée moguls in the early days of her fame, had fatally sapped her *élan vital*. 'She was lazy, spoiled and ungrateful,' complains a producer of an early Bardot comedy. 'She believed that the world owed her a vacation.'

For almost any other future but the movies, Louis Bardot, chairman and managing director of Bardot and Company, one of the largest liquid air and oxygen manufacturers in France, was the right kind of father to have. He was affluent, amiable – although often a little too detached for Brigitte's liking – and very well-connected. He was also a fairly accomplished amateur poet.

Madame Anne-Marie Bardot ('Tatty' to her friends) named her daughter after a favourite doll. Brigitte's early life indeed had distinct doll-like qualities: she dwelled in her own white pastel room furnished with fine Empire pieces and laced finery. A cat called Crocus was her closest companion.

The war, which began a few weeks before Brigitte's fifth birthday, appears not to have touched her very much at all; if the German occupation oppressed and made sullen the polite and proper streets of Passy, it fell short of the nursery door. On the other side of the Seine, across the pont D'iena, the Nazis made their daily noon parade, the band mocking the captured capital with *Deutschland, Deutschland Über Alles*. But she was a child; it was simply another parade witnessed with the feasible discharge of childhood. Her parents were too smart to inculcate in her the rhythms of hate and prejudice.

In spite of the occupation, the Bardots succeeded in giving Brigitte an education that exactly befitted their position in life, a position which Brigitte was naturally expected to accept and duly consolidate in pragmatical and seemly wedlock. The plausible air of snobbery, the protective coating of the French *bourgeoisie*, permeated her whole childhood, creating that cruel loneliness of the over-sheltered and under-fussed child.

'I had a nurse when I was very small and later came a governess,' Brigitte recalls now. 'I saw my parents rarely, very rarely. I suppose I thought they loved me. But it was not exactly the practice we had in the family, you know, showing very much what you felt. My parents are very English in that way.

'I didn't know a lot of children. My mother wanted me to meet and be friends with only those children inside a certain class and up to a certain standard.'

If Brigitte was being turned into a well-educated, cultured and rather boring young lady, she was also intensely curious about life on the other side of the fence. 'I wanted to see what was happening in other families. I wanted to know children of another class and another background. I wanted to know how other people behaved in their homes,' she remembers. But the cause was without a rebel: Brigitte in childhood stayed politely acquiescent.

A businesswoman in Reims who went for a time to the same private school in Paris with Brigitte says, 'I was a prefect in a class or so higher than Brigitte but I recall her because she was a very nice dancer and I too wanted to be a dancer. Most of us realised how hard life was then but always Brigitte seemed to be unaware of the difficulties around us.' She recalled a story about a little rich girl asked to write an essay on poverty; she wrote, 'The family was very poor. The father was broke. The mother was broke. The butler was broke. The cook, the maids, the tweenies, the gardeners and the chauffeur were broke . . .'

It is a story that reminds her always of Brigitte at school. Yet without the future fame to illuminate her anonymous past it is doubtful whether Brigitte would have been much remembered at all; she was, in fact, one of those unspied in-between girls, neither pushy nor a shrinking violet. 'She is,' one benevolent end-of-term report settled for, 'an unopened rosebud

'She has this great . . .*indifference*,' recalls another early acquaintance, 'as if she knew damn well that whatever happened Pappa could take care of it.'

Anne-Marie Bardot's friends complimented her on her quiet, dutiful, well-mannered daughter – 'such a *pleasant* little lady' – searching for nice things to say in the difficult and challenging absence of beauty in the child.

'Brigitte,' confirms a classmate at Madame Bourget's respected ballet school, 'was plain in the most unpromising way.' She wore wire-rimmed spectacles, Victorian hair-ribbons, and kept a brace on her protruding untidy teeth so long that it permanently exaggerated her mouth, fortuitously moulding the now famous pout. 'She also happened to be one of the best pupils in the school. Despite her looks I almost envied her.'

Only in Brigitte's dancing was there real boldness, a magnanimous daring, and something close to passion. Sensually unaroused, not much interested in sport, afraid of horses, she unleashed her energies with tyrannical clout in hard-grind ballet workouts. Old Madame Bourget adored her, predicting a dazzling future in classical ballet. 'I would have remembered Brigitte even if she had never become Bébé,' she once proclaimed. 'She had something that made you soon forget she was not a pretty girl. When she was dancing she had a wild memorable beauty. In repose, her humility had a peculiar grace.'

Brigitte's impressive impact on the ballet teacher was not accidental. 'I knew I was ugly,' Brigitte reflects now. 'I was by nature very frozen, a solemn kind of child. Soon I said to myself: "You must at least be amusing, the best at something, or interesting, otherwise you will be nothing!" I knew I wanted the world to know about Brigitte Bardot.'

'Mama don't Allow . . .'

CHAPTER 2

IF THERE WERE seismometers to detect the first natural tremors, the *causa causans* of legendary stars (those, that is, who are not the fleeting molten frauds of studio production lines) then the needles would have surely quivered in the summer of 1948.

Madame Anne-Marie Bardot opened a small boutique. At first glance, it was not the most propitious time to engage in the frivolities of fashion. The bleak postwar years were not over by a long chalk. Much was still rationed in France, including petrol, and coffee and butter often unobtainable even with the vital coupons. But to the foreign traveller at least Paris was beginning to regain some of its old magic.

Le Hot Club de Paris, the Jockey Club of *Swingue,* put on some spectacular jazz concerts (*La Grande Semaine du Jazz*) with exciting new French stars like Claude Luter and trumpeter Aimé Barelli to be heard alongside Dizzy Gillespie and Coleman Hawkins and other big names from the States. The new bebop sounds and acts like *Les Frères Jacques* were awakening the basement *boîtes* and nightclubs on the Left Bank. Juliette Greco reigned in St-Germain-des-Prés, revered by Camus, Cocteau and Sartre. Mistinquette was still showing her legs to admiring crowds in the music halls.

The Faubourg St-Honoré merchants were slowly filling their

windows with seductive tourist bait. But more than anything else in that flat grey year, Paris had a kind of hypnotic nostalgia for the world. And the fashion scene with its own ghostly drawing cast of classic couturiers and perfumers – Chanel, Worth, Elsa Schiaparelli, Paul Poiret, Coty – gave an aura of continuing glamour to the city. 'In the beginning,' said one French treasury official, 'we must get fashion flowing again; the economy will build from there.'

Anne-Marie's boutique was not, perhaps, such a bad investment. Tourists were again tramping the boulevards; there was the biggest invasion of Americans since the great dollar sprees of the gay 'twenties. Her small stake in the critical fashion world, considerably enhanced by her respectable social pedigree, gave Anne-Marie access to the top people in the business. When millinery designer Jean Barrate was stuck for a theme for his first postwar collection, Mme Bardot was in a position to be heard. She suggested he use a ballet motif. As an apparent afterthought, she nominated Brigitte as his model.

Barrate was apprehensive, perhaps feeling even a little lumbered, when he first met Brigitte. When she danced for him he was enchanted. Rosine Delamare, now one of the leading fashion designers in French movies, remembers seeing that first public performance by Bardot who modelled Barrate's millinery dancing to the strains of *Swan Lake*. 'I thought she was charming. She had a curious defused quality difficult to define. There was no sexuality and therefore, I suppose, no danger. Women could admire her without feeling threatened as they do now.'

'It was,' recalls a fashion writer on the same track, 'like admiring the magnificent lines of a hammerhead shark from behind bullet-proof glass.'

At fourteen, Brigitte appeared to move in a kind of lucid isolation. 'Men seemed to look right through her,' Mme Delamare resumed her reminiscences. 'A friend of mine urged her husband, a photographer, to use Brigitte as a model. He told her, "But she doesn't interest me at all." It was very strange, no, that a man in his business couldn't see the potential, could dismiss her so easily?'

Ironically enough, but maybe predictably, it was a woman who recognised Brigitte's possibilities. A few weeks after the successful Barrate show, a fashion editress who had seen Brigitte's debut needed a teenage model rather fast. The model she had booked for the session had gone down with measles. The editress telephoned Anne-Marie, explained her dilemma, and asked if she might 'borrow' Brigitte when she had finished school that afternoon. The woman was a distant cousin of her husband, a sufficient commendation, and Mme Bardot consented.

A few weeks after these pictures were published in the Junior Miss pages of *Jardin des Modes,* the influential fashion magazine *Elle* asked Brigitte to model for a cover picture. It was a surprising choice. Brigitte, even in the eyes of her most loyal admirers – and they were largely family – still lacked any popular or prescriptive beauty. Hollywood, then a transcendental influence on man's judgement of *le beau idéal,* was firmly decreeing only two looks that year: the Raymond Chandler-sharp, silken-gowned sophistication of Rita Hayworth; and the Weetabix-wouldn't-melt-in-her-mouth appeal of Jane Wyman. Neither of these polarised profiles could quite accommodate the primordial aspects of Brigitte Bardot.

Nevertheless, Brigitte was 'exactly the kind of *gaminerie*' *Elle* needed for that issue.

Mme Bardot was troubled: it was all very well permitting her daughter to help out a relative in a fix but what would her husband say if Brigitte became a recognised cover girl? The naively emotive word model, had a dubious ring in the genteel

Passy society of that time, and maybe still has.

But the *Elle* editors, shrewdly and professionally anticipating resistance along these lines, promised there would be absolutely no publicity, and no fee – an inspired piece of Gallic prudence improbably devised to preserve Brigitte's august amateur status. Moreover, the editors ended their pitch, Brigitte would not be identified by name – 'we shall simply use her initials.' Mme Bardot was reluctantly won over.

One thing is certain. Brigitte had no desire to be a model. The *Elle* cover picture pleased her immensely, of course. She actually stage-managed a series of perplexingly snaky walks with friends from Hattemer's, one of the best private schools in Paris, simply to pass the maximum number of news-stands displaying the magazine. Still her most earnest ambition was to be a ballerina.

But already her destiny was inexorably slipping into new hands.

Roger Vadim Plemianikoff, a handsome young sweet-talking son of a White Russian diplomat and self-proclaimed collateral descendant of Genghis Khan, had seen the photograph. He tore the cover off the magazine and pinned it up in his room. She was not beautiful, he could see that. And certainly she had none of the showy sensuality of the equivocal high-flying women he was used to mixing with in his world of journalism, the women he met on the fringes of the film business. But the irrevealable 'BB' fascinated him in a most extraordinary way. She had exactly the looks, the tone, he'd imagined for the heroine of a screenplay he had recently written for the veteran producer Marc Allégret.

'Find her,' Allégret told him finally, both quietly impressed and a little tired of Vadim's vigorous and abiding advocacy, 'and I will test her.'

An occasional journalist himself, it was a simple matter for Vadim to acquire the name and address of 'BB' from a contact at the magazine. Very correctly – a rectitude inspired not a little by a tip-off that Mme Bardot was a formidable chaperon – he addressed a note to Anne-Marie. He invited her and Brigitte to an 'exploratory business discussion' at Marc Allégret's apartment near the Champs Elysées.

Brigitte was flattered, curious, and keen to pursue the invitation; Anne-Marie felt that the game was moving too fast, and perhaps getting out of hand. She frankly did not want her daughter to become mixed up in movies. Film people, she felt sure, lead very shallow lives. Brigitte had a promising future as a ballerina, why risk that?

By now, however, Brigitte was beginning to show her verve, if not her bursts of ungovernable temper. After several days arguing the toss, Anne-Marie agreed to the meeting. Privately, her strategy was clear. She had decided to play the heavy mother to the hilt. A maternal insolence, she trusted, would dissuade the film men from pursuing her daughter further. The ploy, recalls Vadim, almost worked.

Allégret, a highly professional film maker with a fine record and a respectable reputation for creating charismas (he started Simone Simon on her travels in *Lac aux Dames* the year Brigitte was born) was intensely irritated by Mme Bardot. She dominated the meeting. Brigitte, saying very little, sat with her hands held in the lap of her neat dress with finishing school symmetry. Much to Anne-Marie's disappointment and surprise, the film producer decided to test Brigitte – urged on by the still-vehement and sold Vadim.

The test was not a success. A nervous skin condition erupted on the day the film was shot. Moreover, Brigitte's suspicion of puppy-fat was not entirely disguised by her fine dancer's grace. Allégret felt he had allowed his own judgement to be too easily swayed by Vadim's enthusiasm. 'She talks,' he turned on Vadim, 'as if she is wearing her mother's dentures. And I loathe the way she laughs.'

That might have been the end of it; only Roger Vadim Plemianikoff couldn't dismiss Brigitte from his mind quite so easily. She was, he now believed, the incarnation of the heroine of an unfinished novel, *The Wise Sophie*, he had written as a schoolboy. 'Even the way she spoke . . . it was as if she were speaking straight from the pages of my story!'

There can be little doubt about the quaint impact Brigitte had on Vadim; it amounted to an obsession of almost epic size. Vadim, a ladies man renowned for his cryogenic cool, was truly smitten. (He was never convinced that Bardot, even in the light of the dramas to come, was as greatly involved with him. 'Here, in order after Clown (a cocker spaniel), is what Brigitte likes most in the world: other dogs, birds, the sun, money, the sea, flowers, period furniture, grass, kittens and mice,' he once wrote, adding, 'I did not dare ask her where she placed me – perhaps between the grass and the kittens.')

Brigitte's well-bred almost perverse innocence, her soft credulity, tantalised him. Not only was she a virgin – her interest in boys until the advent of Vadim was minimal – but 'she actually believed that mice laid eggs!,' recalls Vadim.

'It would be fascinating,' he teased Mme Bardot, 'to take your daughter and make it seem as if she has gone completely off the rails!'

Queen Elizabeth II talks to Brigitte (flanked by Dana Andrews and Ian Carmichael) at the 1956 Royal Film Performance.

Former French Premier Edgar Faure is held to ransom for tombola tickets at the Etoiles Fair in 1955. The beautiful brigands: (l to r) Leslie Caron, Brigitte Bardot, Francoise Arnoul.

Cannes Canon fodder: an early Bardot study.

The young Bardot at a dance class.

Pensive study of the youthful Bardot in Rome – where she shared an apartment with another aspiring young actress: Ursula Andress. They have remained close friends.

Before too many cooks . . . Jacques Charrier tries some home-made *ratatouille* on his newly-acquired bride.

Tea with Monsieur Plemianikoff

CHAPTER 3

IT WAS EASIER to see what Brigitte Bardot saw in Roger Vadim Plemianikoff than what he saw in her, an immature schoolgirl, an unprepared woman. Vadim had charm, intelligence, and a past you could steal untampered for any hero in a woman's magazine. His father, a handsome libidinous White Russian officer, fled to Paris after the revolution and married a minor French beauty. A near concert-standard pianist (he had studied at the Warsaw Conservatoire), he made a meagre living playing background music in nightclubs and bordellos in the St-Germain des Prés quarter.

In 1922, he became a naturalised French citizen and soon acquired a modest consular appointment in Alexandra. Vadim was born in 1928 in Paris. His formative years, lived in various consulates (his father held appointments in several parts of Turkey and Egypt), were exotic and precocious.

In Turkey in 1934, during some small political altercation between the two countries, Vadim and his younger sister were kidnapped from the consulate and held captive for twenty-four hours. Fortunately, the kidnappers' hearts were not in it. (Turks spoil their children nearly as much as Americans do theirs.) The tiny hostages were given the best beds and more chocolate than they were ever permitted to eat at home. The following day the

little Plemianikoffs were returned unharmed. Vadim doubts
whether any concessions or lira were extracted in return.

By all accounts, not the least his own, Vadim was a brilliant
child. At the age of six, he wrote a story called *Macrobi*. 'It was
the name of a special gas I'd dreamed up. You put it in a tube and
by reaction it drove the tube forward – in fact, I'd just invented
the jet! My gas was used to drive a train that travelled so fast it
arrived at the station before the sound of its own warning whistle.
It seemed to me wholly logical.'

As a consulate child, Vadim had a rare, insightful, educative
view of humanity from the pomp of visiting dignitaries to the
pathos of distressed travellers brought down by the vagaries of
conmen, pickpockets, riots and Eastern epidemics. His early years,
he remembers with satisfaction, prepared him well for almost any
kind of future.

But the good days for the Plemianikoffs ended suddenly,
without omens, in 1936. While in Paris preparing to take up a
new appointment in Israel, Vadim's father died of a heart attack.
It was a drama fit for the stage: three days before, his life insurance
had run out . . . and had not been renewed. 'The war was coming,
we had no money. We had real problems,' recalls Vadim.

But Mme Plemianikoff was a resourceful, imaginative woman.
'If we are to be poor then let us be poor in the best places, let us
be poor in at least a little comfort,' she told Vadim. They left
Paris and went to the South of France, finding a cheap peasant
cottage a few miles outside Cannes. Having thus escaped from
the congealing squalor of tenement poverty, Vadim developed a
deep respect for penury *al fresco*. 'I learned to ski, to live with the
sun and the earth, I learned about good cheap wine, and cheeses,
all the sustaining simplicities and pleasures of life.' He plays down
the harder moments. 'The wolf was at the door so often,' Raoul
Levy, a producer, once remarked, 'he had to forge a dog licence

to stop getting arrested.'

Mme Plemianikoff remarried; the family returned to Paris. In 1943, Vadim was entertaining vague notions of becoming a diplomat like his father. But his mother, a frustrated actress, ironically urged him to become an actor. He landed an assistant stage manager's job at the Sarah Bernhardt Theatre in Paris. It was a short-lived appointment for reasons now obscure. He didn't learn a lot about acting, but he did discover how much he liked actresses. What was even nicer, they liked him too.

This peculiar and fateful affinity was first celebrated when he was seduced, aged sixteen, by an actress in a Normandy hayloft at precisely the moment the D-Day barrage opened up, giving them both a very unusual experience.

When Vadim met Brigitte in 1949 he was exceedingly well experienced, confident but still without the professional recognition he considered to be his due. He was beginning to be handsome in that tired, seen-it-all style the French admire so much, the look embodied in national heroes from Jean Gabin to Jean-Paul Belmondo. (In London, however, those unaware of French tastes, mistook Vadim's low-key charm – perhaps a little too low-key for his still unforesaken falsetto profile – for something else. He was unkindly christened Goofy, after one of Mr Disney's less alive characters.)

After the failure of Brigitte's test for Marc Allégret, Vadim's enthusiasm for her began to die a natural death. It was not surprising. Mme Bardot was still protectively putting out a lot of domestic propaganda on the impropriety of a cinema career. Vadim, after weeks of some closeness to Brigitte coaching her for the ill-starred screen test, was himself despondent. Brigitte returned to the clasp of education, made tolerable by the daily relief of ballet lessons.

Vadim was being slowly and surely squeezed out of Brigitte's life. And as Anne-Marie was rebuilding her confidence, quietly satisfied she had successfully calmed the unnatural disturbance in her well-ordered household, so the creator of this havoc was sliding into a mood of Slavic despair: 'flirting,' he admits now, 'with the idea of death.' Fortunately, the flirtation was mild enough for him to seek some rallying companionship before the crisis went too far.

'I telephoned some friends and they were not in; I called another number and there was no answer. I was very lonely. I called Brigitte. It was as if I had been pushed to call her: all the other doors were closed.'

Brigitte answered; she invited him to tea.

Brigitte's maternal grandmother, minding the Bardot sisters (Mijanou was born in 1939) during their parents absence in Biarritz, was appalled by the unkempt visitor who arrived that afternoon. Vadim, somewhat ahead of fashion, wore no tie, no socks on his sandalled feet, and hair several inches longer than was considered proper by respectable society then.

'Watch the silver,' the grandmother warned the staff.

He kept his hands off the silver but found it increasingly difficult to keep them off Brigitte. Whether the emotional ordeal of the past months changed the personality of Brigitte's sexuality is both problematical and credible. Certainly Vadim found her more receptive, more congenial than in their earlier encounters. She was just sixteen-years-old when they became engaged.

The love of Brigitte for Vadim appeared to be such an abuse of fortune and breeding that her parents could only ascribe it to a kind of aberration, perhaps some form of passing puberal insanity. Defensively, playing for time for the fever to end, they politely but firmly refused to take the engagement seriously. They pointed out that she hadn't got her *bachot*, the French equivalent of the English General Certificate of Education at ordinary level. But

30

Brigitte cared little for the diplomas and illuminations of life; she never did pass a single academic scholarship in all her girlhood.

Sensing that their careful policy of *pish! tush! tut!* was leading to disaster, the Bardots changed course. Firmly they now told their daughter that she must wait at least two years before 'taking such a serious and irrevocable step as marriage to that most unsuitable boy.'

Brigitte's festering pessimism about the future became pernicious. She began to show signs of the intense emotional instability that was to plague and threaten her life for years to come. Not long ago, Vadim came across a bundle of the letters they sent to each other at this time. Brigitte always returned his letters for safe-keeping, nervous that left in her own possession her parents would discover them. In one of these letters he wrote to her:

> 'You must understand that your parents really do love you but they are scared I am not going to make you happy because I have no situation and no money. Don't be afraid. It will be all right. I promise you. Vadim.'

Brigitte's ominous vulnerability and facile restlessness came out of her innocence: neither her mind nor her body had reached maturity and her anguish and heartache together threatened her constantly. It would be profitless to speculate concerning the outcome – the direction and terms of Brigitte's future existence – if she had been capable of a more profound self-forgetting love at that time. Brigitte Bardot is a woman who never could, and never will be able to pine in obscure and muffled lament for any man. Today she expresses her philosophy with piquant brevity: 'I think like Napoleon: when in love the only victory is to . . .' she jacks her arm and whistles in an unmistakable French gesture '. . . escape, no?'

But in the early 'fifties, Brigitte was a long way off such

gravelled lore. She regarded her parents' attempts to stop the marriage to Vadim as more *bourgeois* snobbery, part of the same nursery code that insisted she made friends with 'only those children inside a certain class and up to a certain standard.'

In the autumn of 1952, Vadim was sent out of town on an assignment for *Paris-Match*. It was a weekend. The Bardot family decided to tour the city's floodlighting spectacle, then still a novelty in postwar France. M Bardot drew up a route that would take in Notre Dame, the Arc de Triomphe, the Palais Royal, and the Opéra. Allowing for the traffic, and dinner in a mid-town restaurant, Louis Bardot calculated the whole exercise would take a little less than four hours.

Brigitte, whose capacity for boredom was already marked, pleaded a headache; she preferred to stay at home, she said. The family left without her.

It was a cold night. Not long after they set out, Brigitte's little sister Mijanou wanted to return to the apartment for a warmer coat.

The apartment was thick with gas. Brigitte, her head on a cushion inside the oven, was already unconscious. The terrible numbing realisation that she was prepared to die from a force of passion shook even Vadim. 'Fifteen minutes more,' he reflects, 'and she would have been dead.'

'Brigitte had virtually announced she would be either wed or dead before Christmas,' recalls an intimate of the family. 'It was a cruel threat but, by god, she meant it.' Not so, insists one long-time Bardot associate. 'She was more interested in the *coup de théâtre* than the *coup de grâce*.'

But the risk was too great to take again. There clearly was no longer any choice. Out manoeuvred and obsessed with the proprieties, the Bardots gave their daughter the requisite smart, if naturally strained, wedding, a honeymoon in the Alps, a small

Son Nicholas makes his debut before the cameras with his mother 48 hours after his arrival in January 1960. 'Do you want more children?' asked a reporter. 'No, no, a thousand times no!' said Brigitte.

Knowing where he stands ... young Nicholas Charrier tries a trampoline in the garden of his father's Riviera home at Port Grimaud.

Bardot, with her little sister Mijanou, on a shopping expedition in Rome. Her chill saved Brigitte's life.

Father of the star: M. Bardot on his way to Brigitte's birthday party in Paris.

apartment in the suburbs of Paris, and a second-hand motor-car.

Brigitte Bardot and Roger Vadim Plemianikoff were married on the 20th December 1952 in the catholic church of Notre Dame de Grace in Passy in the 16th Arrondissement of Paris. Those at the wedding admired the handsome couple. Vadim, perhaps too conscious of the near-tragedy that brought about this day, smiled severely and held himself with an almost military-bearing that amused those who knew him well. Brigitte looked serene and, it was remarked, grown-up for the first time in her life. It was impossible to even guess at the chimeras of her mind. It was not (and there were plenty of guests at that service who did not hesitate to predict it) to be a flawless union.

The Bardot Body

CHAPTER 4

IT MUST HAVE been hard for the quiet, cultured kindly-faced industrialist Louis Bardot, spare-time writer of poetry, to lose his daughter to the handsome, charming, disturbing man Vadim. Already they had fallen out in the most distressing manner over the younger man's impatience to get Brigitte noticed.

Only weeks before her suicide scare in the autumn of 1952 – a matter on which the Bardots have remained resiliently silent for twenty years – Brigitte had appeared half-naked in a film called *Manina, La Fille Sans Voile* (*Manina, The Unveiled Girl*). A cheap, mild exploitation movie, it was sensibly slashed to a mere fifty-seven minutes in Britain and released (with a 'U' certificate) under the skylarky title *The Lighthouse-keeper's Daughter*.

However, this early uninhibited exhibition of the Bardot body emphasised the extraordinary duality of her life at that time – and the powerful influence of Vadim. At home she continued to be difficult but proper, the respectable daughter of a scrupulous *bourgeois* household. But outside there was no doubt at all that Vadim ruled. It was here, perhaps, that the seeds of 'theatrical schizophrenia' (a not uncommon non-medical condition among actresses) were sown. Years later, long after he had carved the initials BB on the imagination of the world, Vadim told me: 'Brigitte's tragedy is that she just cannot let go of her childhood.

Yet she needs constantly to seduce and scandalise to prove to herself how sophisticated and desirable she is. It is a small problem not unlike a kind of schizophrenia . . .

Louis Bardot had approved the *Manina* contract on the strict understanding that his daughter be 'presented decorously and with due respect for her minority status.' He was appalled when he saw the results. After a sharp determined legal skirmish, several of the more revealing scenes were removed. Now, only weeks later, he was irrevocably surrendering his careful patriarchy to Vadim's rampant, ambitious, frank amorality.

Roger Vadim was born with ambition. At six, he was already dreaming of fame. Now, at twenty-five, he was convinced he had found the exact instrument that would bring him that loitering lustre and glory, and fortune besides – his new bride. Friends thought him crazy. Photographers and newspapermen, colleagues from *Paris-Match*, later to plot and compete for her favours, told Vadim he was hopelessly wrong to think Brigitte was star material. She was heavier then. Despite her soft-cushioned childhood, the round of chic catholic schools, and the refining influences of La Conservatoire ballet classes, critics jibed she still had the vellum-tinted complexion and manners of an 'insolent skivvy'.

Her voice, too, needed to be worked on. It was not smart then, as it is now, to down-grade one's accent and play with the argot of the lower class. Brigitte's vocal modulation was considered by many contemporaries to be less than mellifluous. It had a pitch and a coarseness that seemed to insulate her from her expensive background. 'I don't understand it even now,' says Vadim. 'Nobody but me could see her potential in those days. They all said I was wasting my time.' The memory of Bardot in those tender years is still vivid with him. 'She had her own way of moving. It was *almost* aristocratic and *almost* wanton. She had the bottom of a youthful boy. Physically, as well as psychologically, she was the first star to be truly half masculine and half feminine.'

Despite the sneers and scepticism – and Brigitte's own persistent doubts and natural inertia – all the components were there, awaiting only Vadim's assembling genius. And now he was finally free to mould and cultivate his young wife as he pleased; he had assumed absolute authority and his licentious influence would be truly catalytic. When he had done there would be a chain-store reaction around the globe – a million cut-price imitators, the bargain-basement Bardots. The Vadim-Bardot alloy was to change the very shape, look, consciousness, the resolve and the animus of women in the second half of the twentieth century.

But Brigitte did not share her husband's blusterly confidence in her future at all. It didn't seem to worry her much. From infancy she had existed in the world of the rich and near-rich and there was an airy complacency in her manner that bordered on the unlikeable. It was as if she still believed that whatever happened, daddy – or, now, Vadim – could fix it.

Brigitte was no lover of sacrifice. Despite the distinct lack of funds, she remained an indifferent and unenthusiastic cook, preferring, Vadim recalls, to be taken out to dinner whenever possible. It is difficult to imagine exactly what she thought marriage would give her. Certainly the wintry rigours of life with a hustling, indigent husband seemed to hit her with a rude surprise. Washing dishes, and the domestic sciences, were not her line at all; indeed, it is probable they were alien if not sealed facets of life to her prior to her dramatic decampment from the rarefied existence in Passy. 'I despise cooking,' she told friends in the four-star days to come. 'I never cook now; I'd rather not eat than confront a stove.' Her kitchens contain no cook-books, insists one friend, only Michelin guides.

Vadim felt no scruples about ending Brigitte's ballet dreams in order to direct her unwilling energies to the cinema; he secured for her a series of small roles in increasingly bigger but rarely better movies. In a little more than two years, beginning in the spring of 1952, she appeared in nine movies. 'Don't worry,' Vadim assured her when she questioned the quality of the pictures she was doing, 'just learn. It is not important at the start of a career what you do, so long as you are working.'

Shortly after their marriage, Vadim took a small portfolio of Brigitte's photographs (cadged from the newspaper and *Paris-Match* photographers whom he had persuaded to shoot her) to Olga Horstig-Primuz. A former publicist, possibly one of the best operating in Europe, she had recently become an agent, operating on a small intimate level with a select handful of clients, including the distinguished Edwige Feuillere. 'I liked the look of the girl in the photographs very much,' Mme Primuz recalls now in her Champs Elysées office. Without committing Brigitte to her exclusive list, the agent got her a small role in the Paris stage production of Jean Anouilh's *Ring Around the Moon*.

The play lasted one hundred performances and Anouilh was delighted with her. 'You acted like a dream,' he cabled after the opening night. 'Don't worry about the future. I bring you good fortune.' The critics, while not so grandly guaranteeing her destiny, seemed pleased with her. Mme Primuz put her on her books immediately; they haven't parted since. But Bardot never appeared on the stage again. 'Now,' shrugs Mme Primuz, 'the critics would be waiting for her with machine-guns. She is terrified. There is too much at stake now.'

Mme Primuz took on the delicate task of turning Vadim's high opinion of his wife into practical, negotiable terms. 'Vadim was writing the headlines; Olga was working on the small print. Out of the two, it's the small print that counts every time,' says a French film man. Nevertheless, he recognised the formidable combined vigour and capacity of the duo backing Bardot. 'I knew that if Brigitte had an ounce of talent in that extraordinary body nothing could stop her going right to the top of the heap.' Probably the choice had now been taken from her by the new alliance, but there are still those who believe that without Vadim's relentless chivvying, Brigitte would have quit cold. 'You *will* be a star!', he stormed, as she tried again and again to retreat behind the snotty elegance they breed so well in the private schools of Paris.

There were tears, sulking fits, fights. What Bardot lacked in muscle power – and after more than ten years at the ballet bar that wasn't a lot – she compensated with guile. There were also moments of levity. 'After one big row,' recalls Vadim, 'she pretended to be okay and said, "Oh would you be nice and take the garbage downstairs now, Vadim?" The moment I was at the bottom of the stairs I heard the front door slam and the bolts go on. I was really mad. She had locked me out in my pyjamas.'

Vadim broke down the door. 'She was scared like a mouse, running everywhere. It was such a small apartment, two rooms. There was no place to hide. I caught her and wanted to take her by the feet and beat her silly little head against the wall. But that wouldn't be very civilised. So I threw her on the floor and pulled the mattress over her and jumped up and down on that like Tarzan – no, like the monkey of Tarzan. After that we made love beautifully, of course. A man must be strong with Brigitte. It is a fact she has not had a strong man since me.' (This illuminating afterthought was spoken in the autumn of 1971 when we met in St Tropez.)

Their marriage was volatile, modern and, for a year or two, had moments of intense happiness; Vadim's vices have always made him compulsive company, especially with the opposite sex. No one had ever called Brigitte beautiful before Vadim went to work on her. Now she was beautiful and something more. The tentative tone of her body had gone and so had the laminated politeness that stiffened and spoiled her childhood looks. Her sexuality, released from the standards of discipline imposed by family and teachers, had acquired the directness of a sportsman's handshake that comes without secret grips and pressures. No longer seeking intellectual approval, indifferent to fashionable opinion (she has always maintained a serious deficiency of social adroitness) she grew about her an air of carnal challenge and of danger, too. 'She has never been the kind of woman to stand sentry-go over women's mysteries,' it was remarked on one occasion.

But if Brigitte Bardot were converted ('corrupted might be a better word,' corrected a fastidious Passy matron remembering the demure schoolgirl) by Vadim, she had by now become an eager and knowing accomplice. Today she says of Vadim's role: 'Without him in the beginning I would have died; not my body, my career. But if I had not had something within myself, if I had not created something too, possessed some seed, for all Roger Vadim's wiles I would have disappeared.'

Bardot invented herself, says a friend, and Vadim invented the myth.

'From the moment I liberated Brigitte,' says Vadim carefully, 'the moment I showed her how to be truly herself, our marriage was like a downhill racer.' He had turned the key on the most scandalous sex symbol of the twentieth century, but his dedicated campaign to make her a star still needed luck. The luck came at the Cannes Film Festival in 1953.

Arriving uninvited and still almost unknown, with just three movies to her credit, she was promptly taken up by cameramen looking for Leica and Canon fodder on the Croisette. Her tumbled tresses and general air of erotic *déshabille* – there was about her the akimbo insolence of a woman who won't accept there is a wrong side to any bed – greatly enlivened a rather dull year at Cannes. When her money gave out, and she was preparing to return to Paris, photographers are said to have dipped into their own pockets to keep her at the Carlton Hotel for another week. Even allowing for the notorious stinginess of photographers, it was not such a remarkable act of philanthropy: their pictures of Bardot were breaking all over the world and earning them more money than any of them expected to see out of the festival that year.

Posing, pouting, gate-crashing the best parties, urged on and watched over by Vadim, she upstaged the big names – Lana Turner, Olivia de Havilland, and Sylvana Mangano among them. Brigitte's press coverage was phenomenal. Festival officials were not amused. One organiser publicly condemned 'the cheap antics of a little Parisian starlet of no note'. Bardot has ignored the festival, the most important annual film event in France, if not in Europe, to this day, although she often contrives to reside distractingly close (St Tropez) during its annual run. 'I think,' suggests a writer who knows her well, 'she would be prepared to forget that snub and grace the festival again . . . if they gave her a *Légion d'honneur*, no less and no kidding!'

In the dim twilight behind the blinding flashbulbs of the fame counterfeited on the Croisettes of the world, Brigitte Bardot was growing up, both as a woman and an actress. In 1954, Marc Allégret, who had so cruelly dismissed her first screen test, was searching for an actress to play Sophie, an ambitious starlet-figure in *Futures Vedettes* (*Future Stars*). Vadim, who had worked on the screenplay with Allégret, again promoted Brigitte. Once more, Allégret was impressed with Vadim's enthusiasm and promises that his young wife was no longer the child he had tested three years before. The old director agreed to another test. This time he was convinced and she got the part.

'They hired me for very little but it was enough. I would have done the part for nothing,' says Brigitte now. It was the first reasonable role she had landed. 'Sophie was a girl I understood very well. She wasn't exactly nasty – but she was nobody's fool.'

When the film was finished, Allégret told Vadim: 'She is going places, your wife. Not since Simone Simon have I been so sure of an actress.' Vadim, delighted with his mentor's approval, thanked him.

'Don't thank me,' Marc Allégret said quietly.

'*Leading Lady Approval*'

CHAPTER 5

IN LONDON, THE continuing story of Brigitte Bardot was being closely followed by Betty Box and Ralph Thomas, a highly successful producer-director team. Brigitte, they agreed, was precisely the girl they needed to play a small sexy role in one of their *Doctor* comedies. Miss Box had seen an uncut version of *Manina* – 'Brigitte looked about fifteen and was the sexiest thing I'd ever seen in my life' – and had tried to sign her for an earlier picture called *A Day to Remember*. Perhaps because it clashed with another commitment, or maybe because she had no confidence in her English, Brigitte turned it down. The part went to Odile Versois. Now Betty Box decided to try again. She flew to Paris and met Vadim and Bardot in the bar of the Meurice hotel on Rue Rivoli.

'Brigitte could just about say, "good evening" and "I'd like a whisky, please", in English', remembers Betty Box. Vadim did most of the talking. 'He must have spoken English pretty well,' muses Ralph Thomas. 'He persuaded Betty to pay Brigitte $2500.00 for the picture. We both knew she'd never been paid so much money in her life.'

Before the contract was signed, however, Dirk Bogarde – the star of the *Doctor* movies in those days and with "leading lady approval" written into his contract – flew to Paris to meet

Bardot for himself. 'She was enchanting,' he recalls. 'She was also incredibly assertive. She was still only about nineteen* but she actually taught me a lesson I've lived by to this day.' 'Never,' she told the English actor, 'say: "No, I'm sorry, but . . . " If you don't wish to do something always say simply: "No!" That way people can't work on you.'

'She was very positive,' says Bogarde. 'Not tough exactly, but I think she was more in control of her destiny than most people imagined.'

Married celebrities, like homosexual politicians and drinking priests, must present a carefully untruthful picture to the world; but the high correlation between Brigitte Bardot's private image and public performance was now becoming compellingly marked. 'She was the most liberated female I'd ever met in my life,' says Ralph Thomas. 'She was completely natural, there was nothing confected or contrived or artificial in anything she said or did.'

To the sedated tastes of the English film crew, versed mainly in the Listerine and lozengy ways of domestic sex symbols, Brigitte Bardot literally reeked of sex. According to author Doctor Richard Gordon (who also had a hand in the Jack Davies and Nicholas Phipps' screenplay and was a frequent visitor to the set) Brigitte's distinctive bouquet was caused by overactive endocrine glands. He told producer Box that he had observed the same sweet muskiness only a very few times in his medical career and always on very highly sexed women. 'It was the fragrance perfumers have been trying to capture for years without success,' says Miss Box. (Brigitte is not a heavy user of scent; for a long time she favoured *Jicky* by Guerlain, a subtle girlish scent touched with bergamont and lavender and a hint of Provencal herbs. Mostly now she uses *Monsieur*, a masculine cologne by Chanel.)

*She was 21.

48

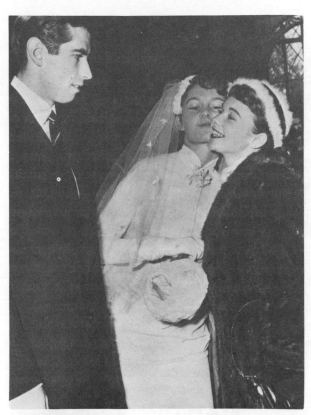

The Vadims' wedding day . . . it was not to be a flawless union.

Another day, another bride

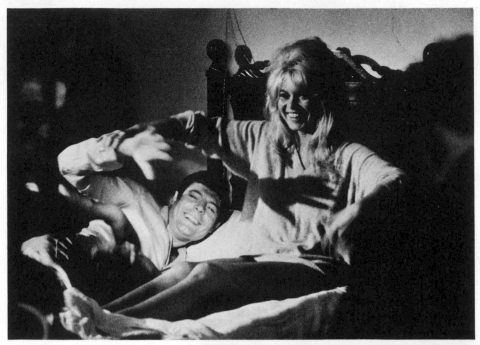

Breaking the tension: Marcello Mastroianni and Bardot romping on the set of *Private Life*. (Director Louis Malle.)

Raincoat romance . . . Bardot and Anthony Perkins rehearse for *Adorable Idiot* in a Paris street.

The Wild One . . . the sex symbol
symbolizing.

In *The Legend of Frenchy King*.

Beauty and the beast: on location in Almeria, Spain. The white Rolls Royce is never far behind . . .

With director Henri Clouzot on the closed set of *La Vérité*: 'My husband,' said Brigitte, 'is such a problem. He is so jealous.'

The film crew, however, had more than mere olfactory cause to remember Brigitte Bardot. 'At that time if you shot a nude scene you'd clear the set of every able-bodied male, leaving a skeleton crew of chaps who were impotent, queer, blind, or generally very ancient,' explains director Thomas. 'Then you'd get the dresser to stick plaster over the actress's nipples and pussy; then you'd shoot her through lace curtains or frosted glass. We had one scene in which Brigitte had to take a shower behind the requisite plastic curtain while Dirk Bogarde sat on the other side, getting hotter and hotter under the collar. Unfortunately, we simply couldn't get the reflection right; however much we adjusted the lights we could clearly see the sticking plaster across her tits and the piece of flannel over her pussy. It looked disgusting. Finally, Brigitte literally screamed *merde*!'

'We've tried it your way,' she told Thomas. 'Now we will do it my way.' She proceeded to peel off the plaster and flannel patties and with a nice smile stepped back into the shower.

'It was considered very daring at that time. She was always very proud of her body. I found her an excessively frank girl; I would have loved to work with her again but we could never afford her a second time,' admits Thomas.

The making of that pleasant, unimportant 1955 British comedy touched Brigitte Bardot's destiny. It was the first time she had been separated from the protection of Vadim's exhortive counselling for any real length of time since their marriage. Her English was severely limited; few people on the set at Pinewood studios in the Buckinghamshire countryside spoke French. To get herself through the peculiarly English script (a maze of mildly sterilised dirty jokes taken at a tantivy gallop) she bought an English dictionary and determinedly and laboriously worked it all out for herself. 'That film,' she was to remark later, 'taught me I could get along by myself if I had to.'

Even so, it now seems that the state of play between Brigitte and her husband had already reached a high degree of per-missive tolerance. Officially, she stayed at the Bull Hotel, Gerrards Cross, during the production of *Doctor at Sea*. 'She thoughtfully left plenty of other numbers where we might find her in an emergency,' recalls Miss Box wryly. However, it seems that Brigitte became quickly bored by British men. Says Miss Box: 'She would say to me, "Betty, what is the matter with British boys? They don't make love?" She took it as a serious personal affront.' ('She didn't say *don't* make love,' is Ralph Thomas' recollection of the conversation, 'she said *can't* make love.')

Bardot's bestrewed open-hearted amiability neither surprised nor hurt Roger Vadim. 'I was rather expecting it,' shrugs the master who has taught his pupil to fly and maybe do it better. His wife, he says, called him constantly from London during that time, pleading for him to join her, cajoling him with memories of past ecstacies together.

'I would prefer to have that kind of woman, knowing she is unfaithful to me, than to completely possess a little girl who just loves me and no one else and has no spirit, no *joie de vivre,* no appetites. I don't want a woman who is prepared to wait docilely, without curiosity, without hunger. That kind of woman scares me, I feel too trapped. If Brigitte had not asked me all the time to go to London, I would have been hurt and unhappy. She was honest and lonely. I knew what was happening . . . but I had things to do in Paris. Important things for both of us.'

Kenneth Green, a brilliant and perceptive publicist, then director of publicity at Pinewood (he labelled her the girl with the pekinese profile; at that time such handles were considered very headline-making) asked her at the end of the picture what she had learned in England during her stay. She said, deadpan:

'The meaning of infidelity'.

Whether or not Bardot and Vadim actually spoke aloud their fears to each other doesn't really matter; each recognised the fact that the marriage was in all seriousness finished. The rift was hopeless. But all that was eighteen years ago; a lot of reflective whisky and water has gone under the bridgework since then. Bardot has created in her own inimitable French style a *ne plus ultra* code of morality that is almost immaculate by the new standards.

'I hate unfaithfulness now,' she told me in Paris in the winter of 1972. 'It is cheap and I loathe it. Yet I also know it is impossible to live always with the same man . . . one day unfaithfulness will happen. That day it is finished, that marriage, that relationship. Another chapter begins. I have had many lovers, yes. But now they are successive. Never do I have more than one at a time. That is enough.'

1955, however, was not the time to rock the gravy-boat, or get too obsessed by questions of sexual ethics and conjugal moralities; Brigitte stayed put with Vadim. By now, certainly, her earlier coolness to stardom had been overcome. She had tasted too much breadline living to pursue her original policy of non-cooperation with her husband's schemes. 'Her decision to stick with Vadim at that time demonstrates very clearly her essential savvy when it comes to matters of business and questions of career,' suggests one French director.

'It was very clear to me that we'd have to split, it was obvious after one year that it was not forever, that marriage,' Vadim says. 'But I didn't want to split until I'd made at least one movie with Brigitte. I felt responsible for her. Because of me she had quit ballet, become an actress against her will. Because of me she had completely changed her whole life.'

Privately, although carefully keeping it from his wife, Vadim was becoming anxious. It had been more than five years since he first started grooming, manipulating Brigitte; she had made a dozen movies including an old-fashioned Hollywood-style epic *Helen of Troy; Les Grandes Manoeuvres* (*Summer Manoeuvres*) for the distinguished René Clair; and Anatole Litvak's *Act of Love,* in which she had one line to speak. Still she had not broken through in the way Marilyn Monroe had in the States. Some seven years older than Bardot, Monroe with little preamble was cutting loose, attracting the finest writers (William Inge; George Axelrod) top co-stars (Laurence Olivier; Robert Mitchum) and the best directors (John Huston; Joshua Logan) in the business. Pushing the same ephemeral stock, Bardot was left way behind. Vadim knew it was impossible to play a waiting game: there is no profit in old-established names in the vital statistics trade. Unless Bardot really took off soon, he fretted to himself, it would be too late.

'She was getting a lot of publicity but people were refusing to take her seriously,' he says. 'Someone had to show what she was really capable of. I knew, finally, I was the only person who could do that. If I had left her then, if we had accepted the end of our marriage, I knew she wouldn't have gone on. All the preparation and sacrifice would have been wasted.

In the summer of 1956, Roger Vadim got his main chance.

Brigitte Bardot was twenty-two.

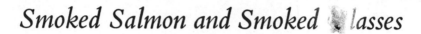

Smoked Salmon and Smoked Glasses

CHAPTER 6

RAOUL LEVY WAS a smart, good-looking, entertaining, very mixed-up social spiv. He had risen from studio floor-sweeper to become a kind of miniaturised Mike Todd-style big-shot of French movies. When success came, he handled it with the showiness of a high-class whore, parading a laurelled and unloved poodle along the best boulevards of Paris. His capacity for the sweet life was infinite and exaggerated and exhibited all the plush and dangerous symptoms of clickola prosperity: his homes in Paris and the South of France had the required acreage of pool (heated, and seldom stirred by anything but the most beautiful bodies) and his walls (including those of his seven-berth yacht) were decorated with canvases by modern masters. He ate smoked salmon for breakfast and wore smoked glasses for supper. His book matches carried his own profile, and he once turned up at a film festival with an entourage that included a dentist to carry out running repairs in his hotel suite. ('La Dolce Vita,' he informed the curious, 'can play havoc with one's cavities.')

In 1956, Roger Vadim completed a script he thought Levy might appreciate; it was called *And God Created Woman*. Vadim's instincts were right; Levy bought it at once. 'Do you have any ideas who should play the girl?,' he asked Vadim. Vadim suggested Bardot. Levy bought that, too. 'It was basically a very bad script,' Levy was to admit later. 'But it had telling accuracy in its observations of how people lived and behaved on the Riviera.'

Despite his honest reservations Levy was convinced of the script's box-office potential. He was astonished to find difficulty getting it financed. After a while, it looked as if the project would have to be abandoned. Levy's backers didn't believe that Bardot's name was big enough to carry the picture. Vadim felt sick; his chance was slipping through his fingers. Levy began uggling the figures in a final bid to present a more attractive budget to the financiers. Vadim suggested he could cut costs even further by letting him, Vadim, direct the movie. He had only one produced screenplay to his credit, *Futures Vedettes*, and had never directed a movie in his life; but he convinced Levy, a man willing to grab at any straw in a storm, that he could handle it.

'It will mean directing your wife in some pretty raw love scenes,' Levy reminded him.

'If I don't know how to direct my own wife in that department,' Vadim answered, 'who the hell can?'

Levy was convinced. The money was pulled together. A young actor named Jean-Louis Trintignant was cast as Brigitte's lover – despite her protests. 'Why don't you find me a handsome boy?,' she demanded, suspecting that Vadim was indulging in some whimsical absurdity. 'Why this boy? He is so odd-looking!'

Trintignant was a little ahead of his time in 1956: he had the face of today, moulded, you suspected, by the mayhem of a lot of yesterdays. 'His face,' Vadim assured his wife, 'is his fortune.' It was rich, Brigitte retorted irritably, only from deposits made by other men's fists!

It was not to her taste at all. Despite his lived-in looks, Trintignant was a gentle unworldly man from Nimes in Southern France. His real ambition then was to be a director; he had taken an acting course at the National Film School in Paris simply to remove an embarrassing provincial accent and to overcome his shyness. The last thing in the world Vadim expected was that Bardot would fall in love with Trintignant. It no doubt came as a bit of a shock to Brigitte, too.

But even if Vadim had anticipated the extraordinary outcome, it is not likely that he would have changed course. He now had the bit between his teeth. Day by day he translated his sensual, accurate screenplay into amorous, shocking and accurate reality, urging his wife to explicit ecstasies, deeper and deeper into the arms of Jean-Louis Trintignant. Often, it was reported from the set, the couple were oblivious to Vadim's cry of 'cut!' at the end of a scene and continued to embrace long after the camera had stopped. ('I never asked Brigitte to be more passionate,' Vadim told me a long time afterwards. 'I asked her to be more sincere. I believe there is a difference. If you go back over my movies, you will find that most of the time passion is a desperate thing anyway.')

Vadim's relentless pursuit of 'total realism' became the talk of Paris. 'He gets so carried away,' Raoul Levy worried aloud, 'he is practically becoming an accomplice in his wife's adultery.' Such thoughts, carefully selected for publication, were not exactly calculated to allay curiosity in his picture, of course.

But even Brigitte seemed surprised how far Vadim was prepared to go. 'Those love scenes became a kind of shameful duel – each defying the other to call it a day,' recalls one of the production members. 'Neither Bardot nor Vadim seemed willing to give way. They were stubborn, wilful or simply very spoiled ambitious people. It was not a good film to be on unless you were a practising voyeur.'

Vadim refutes the idea that he himself has any marked voyeuristic kinks or hangups. 'I simply love it when I am directing a woman on the screen,' he explains. 'Most of the time I direct women I love: on thirteen movies I've made, ten have been with women I was in love and involved with, married or not. But when I begin to shoot a movie it becomes an . . . abstraction. It is like driving a Ferrari at two hundred and twenty miles an hour, it is like putting an aeroplane into a deep dive. It is total cerebration. I can't have an erection on the set when the woman I love is naked and masturbating or making passionate love to another man. It is a moment of – I won't say mysticism because it is too strong a word and anyway people won't understand that – but it's very spiritual. If I were a painter it would be like searching for a new colour, discovering a new texture.'

Brigitte was unaware of Vadim's textural musings (she has very little interest in any metaphysical speculation). Driven to the limits of public passion, she finally walked off the set with Trintignant, the man everybody knew was (or very soon would be) her new lover. 'Like all real killers,' says a friend who saw her go, 'she never looked back.'

'The director won,' producer Levy reflected correctly, 'the husband lost.'

On 6th December 1957 – two weeks less than five years since they were solemnly joined in holy matrimony in the church of Notre Dame de Grace in Passy – they were divorced by mutual consent. The First Chamber of the Civil Tribunal of the Seine, in a nice bit of Gallic understatement, found them equally guilty of 'seriously insulting' each other.

Fifteen years after the notorious *And God Created Woman* was finished, Roger Vadim and I met in the bar of the Victorine Studios in Nice where it all happened. On the wall there still hung a photograph of Brigitte Bardot, wet-lipped and fixed in glossy eternity, looking back across time, congealed in mournful tranquillity. The ups and downs of Vadim's unpredictable course since those early days have done no serious hatchet job on his looks. Standing in the empty bar in the empty studio in the fall of 1971, it was as if we had returned to some ancient battlefield, to Bull Run, to Agincourt or Waterloo, to talk about those who fell that day, to exhume, if not honour, the dead.

'Few things surprise me in this world,' Vadim said, his sad grey eyes like drilled chinks in the armour of his besieged fort of a face. 'But I was really surprised when I saw that little by little Brigitte was falling in love with Jean-Louis Trintignant, especially in view of her original dislike of him.' He seemed a long way off, as if dazed like a reader who looks up after a long session with Bodoni six-point. He lit a cigarette, staring at the photograph on the custard-coloured bar wall. The cigarette hung from his lip. 'Anyway, you know,' he said slowly, his eyes screwed small against the smoke from the Gauloises, 'we both knew our marriage was over and all the problems on the emotional level were solved; but on the sentimental level . . . nothing was solved.' He rotated the whisky glass between the palms of his hands. 'You cannot have seven years in common with a woman you have loved profoundly, and with whom you have a deep understanding, and not feel sad at the death.' ('Vadim cremated his marriage in the heat of those love scenes between Bardot and Trintignant,' an agent once remarked drunkenly at a party. 'Not so,' Vadim is said to have answered. 'I was merely cremating the corpse.')

Brigitte's brief, intense fascination for Jean-Louis Trintignant, a quiet-living actor with a deep sense of professional dedication, revealed something about herself at that time. Friends feared she had become a true penitent, determined to find a lasting saving state of grace and atonement. It was, it transpired in the long run, merely an excessive over-reaction to the years with Vadim. 'I was fighting all the while with Vadim; so many fights. He wanted to introduce me to everyone important. Every night we went out –

to theatres, to parties, restaurants, premieres. It bored me, so much activity. Jean-Louis had other values.' She was impressed with the actor's simplicity and plain-speaking: 'He calls me Brigitte; I call him Jean Louis,' she confided to a friend. 'We don't bother with nicknames for each other.'

She was again showing signs of distinct irritation with the business of acting. 'For me,' she told the same friend, 'art annihilates life.'

She had, by this time, made sixteen movies, none of them exactly a personal triumph and one so cheap the company substituted whitewash for the ass's milk (she was playing the Empress Poppaea) in which she had to bathe.

Her fame, when it came, was swift and surprising.

Eternal Damnation

CHAPTER 7

DESPITE ROGER VADIM'S confidence and the swelling, no longer whispered scandal surrounding its making, *And God Created Woman* did very moderate business when it opened in Paris in November 1956. Producer Raoul Levy, who had borrowed heavily and a little too indiscriminately to get if off the ground, was in trouble. He began to sweat. In December, he flew to New York and offered distributor after distributor the North American rights for a flat $200,000 cash. Nobody would take it. It was felt that the then prevailing censorship strictures would reduce the erotic content to a non-exploitable level.

Brigitte Bardot, who had been paid $15,000 for the picture, the highest fee she had ever commanded, looked as if she had finally come to the end of the road. She simply wasn't box-office; indeed, the first-run Paris take barely topped $125,000—a derisive sum that Raoul Levy bravely dismissed as 'a silly little pimple on the grandeur of my overdraft.'

Now actually face to face with failure (perhaps the one final escape clause in her pact with Vadim) Brigitte was deeply distraught. An actor who encountered her a week or so after the disappointing Paris opening spoke of her 'crumbling voice, her little dismal wound of a face'.

By the early spring of 1957 the overseas receipts started to come in; it was suddenly very clear that Levy had a 'sleeper' – a slow-starting hit – on his hands. Tokyo, Hong Kong, the Middle East, Scandinavia, and finally America and Britain were making a Bébé line for *And God Created Woman*. In Germany, police riot squads had to be called to cinemas showing the picture. In Sweden, a young man overwhelmed by his passion for her while watching the film for the fifth time cut his wrists in the balcony and bled over her admirers in the cheaper seats downstairs.

If it was all so peculiarly dated, it was also the real stuff and nonsense of movie legends, of Theda Bara and Valentino and Clara Bow. Somebody promptly coined the word Bardolatry; distinguished intelligent men (and women, too) began to spout volumes on the revolutionary doctrines and Lolita syndromes explicit in Bardot, the acclaimed avatar of the new free child-woman, the spirit of the era of orgasmic compulsion. But, more to the point, behind the deeply meditative ticker tape being showered upon her from great highbrows, Brigitte Bardot had overnight become the number one sex symbol in the world. ('Most of the nice things that happen to me seem to happen overnight,' she told me when we later met in Mexico.)

Marilyn Monroe, beset by emotional disturbances, constantly fighting the studios, and soon to become the last spectacular victim of the old Hollywood star system, was a dwindling box-office enticement. The future was clear for Bardot.

Raoul Levy signed her for four more pictures, her fee escalating to $25,000 plus a piece of the profits. To celebrate their new partnership (and help spend some of the $2½ million *And God Created Woman* was now projected to earn in America alone) Levy gave her a huge reception at the Venice Film Festival. The old-time hoopla was staggering: three stunt planes doodled the initials 'BB' in the sky, two hundred and fifty guests were given a seven-course dinner in a five hundred-year-old palazzo on the

With Marcel Amont in *La Mariée Est Trop Belle*.

With Jacques Charrier in *Babette Goes to War*.

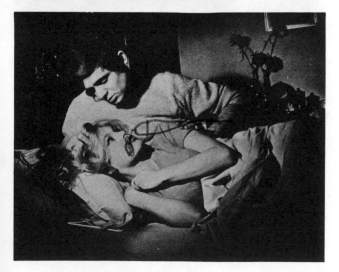

With a new leading man, Charles Belmont.

The Esso sign means happy motoring . . . a scene from *Les Novices*.

Two Weeks in September: playing a bride – but beginning a film for the first time without a husband or lover on tap.

Critics predicted Jeanne Moreau would act Bardot out of sight in *Viva Maria!* . . . Bardot made them eat their words.

Down to the she in sheets . . . with Maurice Ronet in *Les Femmes.*

Grand Canal, art directors were flown from Paris to supervise the decor and flower arrangements. (Raoul Levy would never quite reach those heights again. On New Year's day 1967, six pictures later, aged forty-four, he shot himself dead outside a young model's apartment in St-Tropez.)

'I cannot play roles,' Brigitte confessed what was to become a familiar quote, 'I can only play me – on and off the screen.' Cynics dismissed this shocking candour as merely part of the cunning stratagem, devised by Vadim, to perpetuate the enriching 'sex kitten' image – a dialectically sound combination, analysed one observer, of two very old and surefire appeals: the ingenue and the tramp. Out of the two, the Vatican preferred to believe the latter and duly elected her to symbolise Evil! A cardinal refused to sign the visitors' book in a Bavarian village because his signature would have followed a heart drawn and autographed by Bardot. ('It is nothing personal,' explained Cardinal Doepfner, Roman Catholic Primate of Bavaria, 'but merely a matter of good taste.') And in a rare display of theological *entente cordiale*, Jehovah's Witnesses proclaimed her eternal damnation. 'I've been condemned from more pulpits,' Brigitte shrugged philosophically 'than Satan.'

But if for some she stood for pure muck, for others she represented a kind of modern purity. (Her face and bosom now symbolise the Fifth Republic itself. Sculptor Alain Gourdon-Aslan used her as his model for the official *Marianne* bust without which no French town hall is absolute.) And there were those who felt her commercial triumphs deserved glorification of a kind. 'BB now deserves to be considered an export product as important as Renault automobiles,' wrote Simone de Beauvoir in a celebrated essay in 1959. Bardot agreed. 'It's disgusting,' she lamented. 'Here I am sweating to make one picture in three simply to pay my tax and the government is making millions out of me. I will write to de Gaulle and threaten to stop making films.'

Despite the burdensome taxes, however, she was well on her way to becoming very rich indeed. And sharp with it. She kept a close exemplary watch on the household accounts. A former secretary recalls that she set a top limit of $2.50 per head when entertaining at home, a prudence much admired by the French. Moreover, she invested well – in oil, sugar, property, Nestlé's, the Printemps stores – and is reputed to have thoroughly impressed even the head of the Bank of France with her fiscal perception. 'I am,' she admits cagily, 'quite a rich lady. If I stopped now I would have no problems. I have enough money to live well for quite a long time. But despite some reports, unfortunately, I am not a very good business lady.' 'She knows how to mine from life precisely the things she wants,' admires the English director Ralph Thomas. 'If ever she retires she'll make a great agent.'

Brigitte's agent, however, Olga Horstig-Primuz, insists that her client doesn't have a calculating bone in her body; her business acumen is generated by instinct alone. It was immediately after the runaway success of *And God Created Woman* that the first flushed offers from Hollywood started. One deal, a fat five-year contract with a major studio, was considered by Mme Primuz to be worth accepting. Bardot took her advice with apparent equanimity. A few days before the deal was to be finalised – the contract ran to over one hundred pages – Vadim warned the agent: 'I know Brigitte doesn't want to tell you but she is terrified of the deal. She doesn't want to leave France. She is crying all the time.' Mme Primuz cancelled the contract. It was, she concludes, absolutely the right decision. 'But it was not a hard-headed business calculation; it was a feeling Brigitte had, that's all.'

It had been a tough, exciting, momentous year, 1957. When it opened, it seemed as if Vadim's dreams of making Brigitte

66

Bardot a great international movie star were finally dashed; now, in the closing months, the dream had become reality. In America, after the success of *And God Created Woman* (despite a great deal of censorship surgery, it ran for ten months in the New York art house that had originally booked it for ten days and finished up among the most successful foreign films ever to play in the United States) film men were avidly, almost irreligiously, resurrecting every early Bardot picture they could lay their hands on. Brigitte was suddenly turning up in art houses, neighbourhood family cinemas, and even in 42nd Street grind palaces.

But emotionally Bardot was bankrupt. Her marriage in ruins, Jean-Louis Trintignant called up for his military service, she was for the first time in her adult life without a constant lover. 'She is on her way to becoming a neurotic,' opinioned Raoul Levy. 'She is a very, very sick girl.' She watched with fascination and apparent horror the downhill peregrinations of Marilyn Monroe in Hollywood. 'It happens so fast, so fast,' she repeated sadly. 'Monroe's fate should have been a salutary lesson for Brigitte but she didn't seem to grasp the personal implications at all,' suggests a director who worked with Brigitte in the early days.

So the schizophrenia of stardom got to her. Brigitte was the new goddess on the chopping block: in New York, a store was advertising 'a genuine lock of Brigitte Bardot's hair' for five dollars. The critics, alas, seemed to be more interested in her scalp.

Nevertheless, she was moving into a classier type of picture. She was also getting highly respected co-stars – including the venerable Jean Gabin who enquired when Bardot was first suggested as his next leading lady, 'What? That thing that goes around naked?' The picture was *En Cas de Malheur* (retitled *Love is my Profession* in Britain and America) based on a Georges Simenon novel about an amoral trollop who corrupts and destroys an honorable lawyer. Gabin is understood to have grown to admire Bardot immensely during the production of this picture. Even so, he had to be persuaded with a court order to continue filming after he learned Brigitte was to get equal billing in France and top billing in Britain and the United States.

But again, when the picture was released, critics were not much impressed with Brigitte's acting ability, possibly because the censor had already removed some of her best scenes – including a classic sequence in which she tries to persuade the ageing attorney, played by Gabin, to drop his fees by raising her skirt. The movie was angrily attacked in Paris for its immorality. Still audiences all over the world responded to her emancipated sexuality with enthusiasm.

'In two years,' insisted the London *Daily Herald* in 1958, 'she will be just another continental bosom and wiggle girl. In five years people will be saying: Brigitte Bardot? Oh yes, she was that French girl they used to make all the fuss about!'

It was not such a ridiculous opinion as one might suppose. Despite the evidence of the balance sheets, even close friends suspected that without Vadim around to push her, advise her, love and bully her every inch of the way she would soon be washed-up. Even Brigitte herself had little faith in her staying power. 'In three years time,' she confided to friends, 'I will be ready for the public to forget me – and the public will be ready to oblige.'

She was living her life between bed and bedlam. 'When a man attracts her, Bardot goes straight to him. Nothing stops her. It does not matter if she is in a cafe, at home . . . she goes off with him on the spot without a glance at the man she is leaving,' wrote French novelist Marguerite Duras. 'In the evening perhaps she will come back, perhaps not.'

It was some time before Brigitte recognised that she was a

woman who needed not the flattering parasites, not the cometary enamoratos, but a specific man in her life. Yet no man, husband or lover, has lasted more than three years. During that time, he is the elemental force, the essential conjunction of her happiness. 'I live my whole life around my man – work, play, dreams, everything. My lover is the centre of my existence. When I am alone I am lost. I can find myself only with a lover,' she says. 'Some actors say they can only really exist when they are playing a role; me, I can only play a role – only exist – when I am loved. Outside a relationship I am in space.'

Despite the hundreds of thousands of words in all known languages being churned out about her in the last years of the 'fifties (or perhaps because of them) Brigitte Bardot remained somehow enigmatic, an elusive fugitive in the wilderness behind the glossy frontispiece of her fame.

And she was heading for a crack-up.

Men over Thirty:
'Ready for Chrysanthemums'

CHAPTER 8

IN THE AUTUMN of 1960, on her twenty-sixth birthday, Brigitte Bardot abruptly left a lunch party at a Cap Martin restaurant, drove to the small secluded villa she had rented at Cabrolle, some thirty miles outside Nice, took a bottle of sleeping pills and sliced open both her wrists.

It was the grim finale to three enriching years of frenzied fulfilment, conquests, passions, postponed pain and eluded reality. During that time, beginning with the end of her marriage to Roger Vadim and the simultaneous collapse of her notorious Kleig-lit affair with actor Jean-Louis Trintignant, she sought only the pleasurable moments. Her life was veiled in a nebula of erotic self-centred dramas. Those who could counsel her with the licence of old friendship were becoming fewer all the time. Her weakness for young men was now very well marked: RFC – ready for Chrysanthemums – was her dismissive code for men of more than thirty years, however rich and eligible they were considered to be.

The press watched and reported her every move and dalliance: thus young men like Sacha Distel could walk into her affections unknown and right out the other side veritable celebrities. Distel, who met her in St Tropez in the summer of 1958, recalls now: 'I was just starting out as a singer. My manager warned me it would take a lot of hard work and time before I could expect to make it. Then I met Brigitte – and one week later I was *the* man in the world.'

They were inseparable: the small neat beautiful man, with eyes the colour of *crème de menthe* set in a face tanned to the shade of strong tea, and the beautiful notorious actress. 'We would be married now,' Brigitte told friends, 'but the press are always too close.'

Brigitte and Sacha. Sacha and Brigitte. They were photographed everywhere together. Sunbathing on the Riviera, riding around Paris in his silver Lancia, holding hands in the gondolas on the canals of Venice, playing guitars, dancing, dining, kissing, swimming. Brigitte, the legend goes, proposed to Distel after they attended a friend's wedding which she found intensely romantic; Distel saw no apparent reason to decline her hymeneal invitation and proceeded to serenade her publicly and unabashedly with lilting lyrics celebrating her pout, her smile, her walk and with songs questioning her demoniacal beauty – angel or devil? which is your real face?

Sacha soon found out. She ended the affair six months after it began with a chill and regal communique issued through her private (male) secretary: 'Mlle Bardot wishes it to be known she has broken off all relations with Sacha Distel.'

What, somebody asked Distel when the famous idyll was over, did Brigitte Bardot teach you? Never, he replied, to put your trust in actresses. He married ski champion Francine Breaud, proclaiming her 'sanity'. His chagrin was understandable in the light of his cuckoldom; for some time Brigitte had been playing him off against her new lover, causing embarrassment and nervous speculation among those in the know. 'It was magnificent the way she had them coming and going, often missing each other by a whisker,' recalls an intimate. 'It had all the delicate hilarious timing of the finest French farce.'

Yet it revealed too Brigitte's emotional insecurities, her abiding fear that one day she will be left without a lover at all. Years later she told me: 'I must always have a new lover in sight before I am able to let the old one go. I must always be sure of one. So, of course, there is often this difficult time of change. I cannot live alone, you see. It is stupid but it is like that. I may be emancipated but finally I am not free.' ('I want,' Bardot has told Vadim, 'to finish my life with you. When you are sixty and I am past fifty, perhaps. It will be easier then for people like us.' Vadim is not convinced. 'It can be little pleasure being with a woman once her sex interest has gone. I want to be close to a woman I love and watch the flame die slowly, beautifully. There must be dignity in that final little death. I don't want to be made a present of . . . darkness, a corpse!')

The new man in her life was Jacques Charrier, three years younger than Brigitte, a rising actor and her co-star in *Babette Goes to War*. On 18th June 1959, six weeks after she had publicly dismissed the astonished Distel, Brigitte married Charrier in the village of Louveciennes, home of Louis XV's mistress, Madame Dubarry. M Charrier confessed himself completely bewitched by his bride.

Before the honeymoon was over, Brigitte was pregnant and Charrier had been called up for his National Service in the army.

A jealous, quick-tempered, straight-laced man, full of actors' insecurities and the natural doubts of any who enters marriage so hurriedly, Charrier was distraught and shocked to find revealing pictures of his bride over practically every bunk in the barracks. If he now recognised his bewitching Love Goddess for what she really was, a highly commercialised creature of more earthly substance, it did not end his enchantment, nor ease his pain.

Bardot's condition did not help matters. Not only pregnant, she was also suffering from depression of a kind alleviated only by the actual presence of her husband; her physician sent urgent communiques to Private Charrier's commanding officer explaining the predicament and requesting the new recruit's palliative presence at his wife's side in Paris. The request was granted; several times.

These prompt and ready spells of compassionate leave did not go unnoticed; difficult questions began to be asked in the National Assembly: 'What measures is the government proposing to take to ensure that all recruits are treated equally, even when they come from the arms of a great actress?'

Charrier was admitted to the Val de Grace military hospital, also suffering from nervous depression. Doctors declared he was the victim of 'psychological mistreatment' from other recruits. His military career was coming to an end. After precisely five weeks intermittent soldiering in Orange, Southern France, Private Jacques Charrier was dismissed from the army. His discharge papers bore the legend: *inapte à sirvir*. The son of a professional army colonel, his health, his pride, and his emotions were all broken. He survived two suicide attempts; a year later, he was still having daily psychiatric treatment. 'I knew it wouldn't be easy being the husband of the sex symbol of the era,' he lamented later. 'But I never thought it would be such a trial.'

At 3 am on 11th January 1960 Nicholas Jacques Charrier was born in Brigitte's seventh floor apartment on the Avenue Paul Doumer, near the Trocadero. Sets of clothes identical to those in Nicholas' layette were sent to fifty babies born in Paris at approximately the same hour. Jacques invited the press to a champagne celebration in a nearby café and made all the proud noises of fatherhood: the baby was the most beautiful in the world, weighed six-and-a-half pounds, had blue eyes, possessed a powerful tenor voice exactly like his father's, would be bottle-fed, was delivered by the painless birth system. The nursery was modelled on Brigitte's memories of her own: pale blue walls, white carpet and curtains, a white cot on wheels with a frilly white canopy and an ornate white Second Empire birdcage filled with soft toy animals from Brigitte's childhood. Brigitte, he added, always knew it would be a boy and refused to even consider names for a girl; now she was very tired, but very, very happy.

It was all true except for one thing. Brigitte was not very, very happy at all. By this time it was perfectly clear to friends that the marriage was far from snug. They fought constantly; friends were appalled by Brigitte's impaired appearance during her pregnancy. 'It wasn't a good time for her,' says a girl friend. 'I think they were the unhappiest months of her life. Unfortunately, she couldn't help provoking Jacques. I suppose she can be very annoying sometimes. But he tried to keep her in line with his physical superiority. It was a bad mistake. Brigitte hates violence.'

But aside from the prevailing bleak domestic scene, Brigitte had other reasons to question the joys of motherhood at that time. To a sex symbol, pregnancy is as fraught with risk as alopecia to a pop star. Maternity – the very word, smelling of antiseptic and rubber sheets, was anathema to her – not only threatened her narcissistic brand of happiness, it could put her beyond the erotic dreams of man. She knew that the name of her game was desirability. It's a game that unfortunately doesn't get any easier with maturity.

Brigitte didn't waste a lot of time. Four months after her son was born, she resumed her career with a movie called *La Vérité*.

It was her twenty-fifth film, and potentially it was the best role she had ever had; the director was the acclaimed Henri Clouzot. Shooting started in Paris in May. It was the beginning of the most hazardous six months of her life.

Jacques Charrier, out of the army, and in and out of psychiatric clinics, became ominously jealous of her new leading man, Sammy Frey, despite Brigitte's own initial opposition to him; she had asked for her old flame Jean-Louis Trintignant to play opposite her. It was almost certainly a shrewd feline bid to rekindle the shocking charisma that had been so good for her box-office image in the past. In an early testing trial of strength with the wily director, Brigitte threatened: 'I refuse to rehearse with Frey. It must be Jean-Louis or I will not appear.' But she knew she needed Clouzot more than Clouzot needed her at that moment when her commercial magic was to be challenged for the first time since achieving motherhood and mortality at a single stoke.

The strain between Bardot and Charrier was by now no big secret in Paris. A mineral water company cheekily plastered the whole of France with posters asking, *Bébé aime Charrier?* ('Does baby like Charrier?') to advertise a drink named Charrier. Bardot was not amused. She sued the company, claiming that the question mark implied doubt of her love for her husband. Unfortunately, less than six weeks after this legal declaration of familic harmony, producer Raoul Levy was obliged to hire guards to keep a very irate Charrier out of the studio during his wife's typically explicit love scenes with Frey. 'My husband is such a problem,' Brigitte told me at the time. 'He is so jealous. Especially about my love scenes. And all Henri Clouzot wants to do is make them more . . . how you say? More true, more real.' The sense of *déjá vu* was intense.

It was altogether an extraordinary situation, tinged with the slightly overcranked momentum of ancient Hollywood farce. Charrier, in a grandiose fit of pique, removed himself to a nursing home; Vadim reappeared on the scene, consoling his former wife in her difficult but not unfamiliar situation; Vadim's new wife, Annette Stroyberg, confused, sought advice from Sacha Distel; Clouzot's wife, Vera, apparently distressed by her husband's professional obsession with his leading lady also succumbed to a nursing home; Raoul Levy contemplated aloud his future in the film business and wished his mother had let him play with gelignite as a child.

Then fifty-three, pipe-smoking, reflective and fluent in existentialism and philosophy, Clouzot told me wearily: 'I know that all Paris is talking about Brigitte and me. I've heard the rumours. If she has any affection for me it's as a director or as a father figure. That's all. It just so happens that my wife is sick and in hospital and so is Brigitte's husband. So the tongues wag. But I tell you, my influence over her is only an aesthetic one.'

Brigitte, in public, held herself together very well. 'Inside herself she was all systems go for one almighty crack-up,' Raoul Levy said. 'Awful things were being said about her; she was made to sound like a female Caligua. She was wiped off a hundred guest-lists.' Social boycott is not a weapon to bother Bardot. She belongs to no gang but her own small moveable changing team. ('She thinks the social swim,' observed one ex-lover wryly, 'is mixed bathing in the nude.') Yet the feeling of isolation was growing around her; the threat of depression, constantly close, was moving in for the kill.

In the small hours of a Sunday morning in the middle of September 1960, Jacques Charrier challenged his wife and actor Sammy Frey as they arrived at a fashionable St Germain-des-Prés nightspot called La Rhumerie, noted for its rum grogs. There was an ugly brawl between the two men, greatly appreciated by the Left Bank boulevardiers. Bardot was in tears. One week later, she was found drugged and bleeding in the garden of her rented villa in the South of France.

Her mother flew to her bedside. She was told that Brigitte had taken a serious dose of barbituric 'quite enough to kill her, but for prompt treatment she would have been dead within ninety minutes'. Mme Bardot left the St Francois clinic sobbing. 'Brigitte does not want to live and she will do this thing again.' Later, at a hastily convened press conference, at the Negresco hotel in Nice, Anne-Marie told reporters: 'I beg you as a mother for her life: let her alone and let her live. I know Brigitte Bardot belongs to her public. I know the public and the press have helped her, but now it is not a question of her career, it is a question of her life.'

While Bardot lay in the darkened room of the Riviera clinic, attended by the best specialists in France, fans were ransacking the villa where she had tried to kill herself. Even bloodstained tiles were taken for souvenirs. 'I thought that kind of ghoulishness went out with Valentino,' complained the shocked and in-commoded owner of the looted villa.

Bardot had been playing a dangerous game, of course. An explicit amalgam of redeeming vices, her amorous anarchy became a kind of public light entertainment, a spectator sport, to be reported, criticised, analysed and admired. She was the idol of the mob, the divine object of mass adoration and collective fantasy. She was exposed to a public flattery that virtually eclipsed the lodestar of private affections. She developed about her the smugness of a beautiful woman who has distributed her fine gifts munificently and done her charities proud.

'She sacrificed everything in her private life to sustain the great money-making myth of Bébé,' levels one French publicist. 'Men fall in love with the idea of Brigitte Bardot. When she

A familiar routine . . . with actor J. M. Bory.

A screen test: actor Hugues Aufray goes through his paces.

The PVC of it: Rehearsing with Jean-Pierre Cassel.

With Louis Jourdan in *La Marieé Est Trop Belle*.

Oblivious to the director's cry of 'cut!' . . . one of the love scenes with Jean-Louis Trintignant in . . . *And God Created Woman*. The furore made her.

starts to become a real woman to them, she simply gets rid of them. At all cost, she must preserve the illusion, the mythology.'

The public was genuinely surprised, and the French were offended, when she tried to take her own life. Somehow it was a betrayal of the myth. 'They behaved as if I were some factory going out of business,' Brigitte reflected in the melancholy aftermath, 'I was not human at all, but a convenient public utility they were afraid of losing.'

In 1972, a dozen years after all this, we were talking in Paris when I mentioned that Richard Burton once said he feared dying and being forgotten more than anything else. 'Being forgotten I don't worry about,' she said. 'Everybody is forgotten eventually, the grandest moments are dust in the end. But dying is horrible. There should be another way to end something as beautiful as life. I don't want to know what is going to happen to me next week, tomorrow, not even tonight. But I do know for certain that I must die some day and the future is death. That frightens me a lot.'

I reminded her of her own attempts on her life. 'Yes, but why?' she said. 'Maybe at that time I thought: "Well, I have to die sometime, so why not now? Why work and suffer and be unhappy? If once you have to die, what is all this stuff before?" I like sometimes to get things done with.' I asked whether she felt that suicide was still on the cards for her one day. 'I think now it's over, that phase,' she answered slowly. 'I tried it and it was not a success. And I hate failure.'

But, as Graham Greene has written somewhere: 'failure, too, is a kind of death.'

In 1960, Brigitte set out to cauterise her wounds with a series of affairs; she seemed to pick on men who were younger, poorer, far less successful than herself, men with nothing to lose and everything to gain.

Olga Horstig-Primuz chided her for her apparent arrested taste in men: she seemed oddly obsessed for a time with the kind of muscled sportsmen you find upside down on their hands along hot beaches. Brigitte was amused by Mme Primuz's concern, and unrepentent. 'But I've always adored pretty young men,' she said. 'Why should my taste change simply because I'm a little older?'

Mme Primuz, who probably understands the star as well as any woman ever will, says now: 'She has a predatory sensuality. At heart she is a little *mec*. She knows only how to play the male role in a relationship; she makes the running and the decisions. So she is attracted to weaker men; but they say opposites attract and it is very possible she has no choice.

'I think at the bottom of herself she is not a gay person, she is a sad lady, moved very easily to melancholy. Most people, you know, find their happiness in short moments and pretend it is long: Brigitte does not bother to pretend.'

Alleging the now familiar 'serious insults' Brigitte was divorced from Jacques Charrier in January 1963; custody of their two-year-old son went to the father. 'I think I'm not made to be a mother. I don't know why I think this because I adore animals and I adore children, too, but I'm not adult enough – and I know it's horrible to have to admit that at thirty-seven, I'm not adult enough to take care of a child" she told me when we met in Madrid in the fall of '71. 'I need somebody to take care of me! It's such a big responsibility to have a baby. Life is so hard now, we don't know what is going to happen to the world tomorrow, or even in the next hour.' Her voice faded a little bit, like a radio badly tuned. She mumbled something that I didn't catch. Then she said very evenly in a small voice, 'I'm very sad to have had that baby – well, he is not a baby now, he is twelve years old. What will be his life? People who are making babies and families now are mad. It is such a bad world.'

I was surprised a little after she told me this to notice that her name was missing from a high-powered public petition to legalise abortion in France. 'A million women have abortions every year in France. I declare that I am one of them.' Jeanne Moreau, Catherine Deneuve, Simone de Beauvoir and Francoise Sagan were among those who signed that confession – making them all liable to a heavy fine and up to two years in prison. 'Was it possible,' mused *Time* magazine, 'that Brigitte Bardot had not had what Simone de Beauvoir had?' There were, it seems, 'intimate personal reasons' why she didn't want to sign the petition. She offered the movement money instead.

No Time to Put His Cock On . . .

CHAPTER 9

COUNT GUNTHER SACHS von Opel, Brigitte Bardot conceded after the lawyers had thrown the dust sheets over their marriage, appeared to be the ideal man for her. And ideal men are hard to come by when you are a rich famous woman with a past, and a will of your own. 'Gunther had all the attributes, he was even richer than me!' she reiterated in amazement.

In fact, Gunther Sachs, as he prefers to be known, seemed almost too good to be true. He was that rare breed of millionaire who actually takes pleasure in spending his money, particularly when he is spending it on beautiful women. Moreover, he was handsome, free, amusing, and in fine shape with that always-tanned look of professional sportsmen and Mediterranean yacht skippers. He was a favourite subject for tittle-tattle and speculation in the best salons and the worst gossip columns of Europe and had gathered an immodest reputation as a playboy, an epithet he accepts still with aggrieved dignity. He naturally inspired the rumours and illusions his kind have always inspired; even when the stories are not true they create auras of sensual tension and mystery about their victims. Gunther's notoriety, Brigitte reflected with amused satisfaction, almost matched her own. His growing reputation as a kind of high society sex symbol fascinated her a great deal.

But there is rather more to Count Gunther Sachs von Opel than that. His story is the stuff Harold Robbins gets rich on in no few words.

Gunther was born in Germany in 1932; his mother came from the famous old Opel motorcar family; his father ruled an engineering empire, specialising in engine accessories, which Gunther was to inherit with an older brother. His early education, you might think, was a bit handicapped by the emphasis laid on such matters as bobsleighing (he became European Champion in 1958), golf and shooting. He appeared to show no remarkable intellectual bent. He was also fond of fast cars and, from an early age, the kind of women who decorate them very nicely.

At twenty-two, however, he showed sudden signs of settling down to more serious study. He acquired a place at the University of Lausanne. He was, suspected older members of the family, now ready to prepare himself properly for the heavy responsibilities to come.

At Lausanne, he met a French student named Anne-Marie Faure. She was beautiful, amusing, intellectually stimulating. They fell in love. His parents, displaying the German aristocrat's native dislike and suspicion of the French, were far from satisfied with the proposed union; they told Gunther he would have to wait two years before they would consider giving their approval to the marriage. Showing commendable restraint and filial obedience, Gunther bided his time; he finally married Anne-Marie in 1954. A little less than one year later, a son, Rolf, was born. It was, by all accounts, a splendid happy family. In 1957, Anne-Marie underwent a minor operation; it was not considered to be at all serious only complications came and she died, aged twenty-five.

For a while, Gunther attempted to forget his shocking grief in work. 'He became obsessed with business,' recalls one associate.

In the beginning suitor Bob Zaguri had plenty to smile about.

Bardot, bouquet and beau from the past . . . acha Distel.

With Christian Kalt, a durable liaison, in St. Trop.

A reflective moment at the Paris premiere of *Bulliit:* with Patrick Gilles. He followed Gunther.

With personal photographer Jicky Dussart.

Barefoot in the dark: Bardot leaves a Riviera nightclub with English chum Christopher Lance.

Sex kittens, like leopards, don't change their spots. With Eric Salmon nowhere near 'ready for chrysanthemums'.

Bardot quietly rebelled against Gunther Sachs' highlife – like arriving at the celebrated Maxim's in Paris shoeless.

Two of a kind: Bardot and Hollywood sex symbol Mr Warren Beatty.

A Certain Smile from novelist
Françoise Sagan.

Michael Sarne: rendezvous in
Chiswick High Street.

'It began to threaten his health. Friends became concerned. Finally his family urged him to take some time out, to relax, to travel.' Gunther was persuaded. During the next six months, he travelled to most of the playground capitals of the world. 'Anne-Marie's death,' said one of the Jet Set he had so fatefully joined, 'put him on a crash course in the practical technicalities of hedonism.' Even so, he had been preparing for it all his life.

Not a man to indulge in self-pity or those emotions which sometimes pass for self-analysis, Gunther embarked on a series of grand romances. Each relationship cheerfully and graphically chronicled in the press. Princess Soraya and Tina Onassis were among the international beauties reported to be engaged to him – at separate times, be it said. In St Moritz he met Birgitta Laaf, a stunningly attractive model. They became engaged: Gunther, said his friends, was truly happy again. It even looked as if he would settle back once more into a life-style of tranquillity and social repose.

The couple repaired to his sumptuous Bavarian chalet to plan their nuptials. Then Birgitta collapsed with a spinal tumour. Paralysed, unable to leave the chalet, visitors were touched to see Gunther carrying Birgitta in his arms like a child. It was some time before the determined millionaire found a surgeon confident of curing the crippled girl. The operation was a success. But the ordeal had been too much for both of them and they parted soon after Birgitta learned to walk again. 'Like the *Bismarck*,' admired an old accomplice, 'Gunther has broken out.' The hunt was on once more: the perfumed fleet of desirable and determined women set out to get him in their sights. It was a sport at which the millionaire excelled. 'Women are the most divine creatures in the world,' he answered when sober business associates grew impatient with his dalliances. Like his friend Roger Vadim, women had the same invigorating almost reverent effect upon him as driving fast cars or doing the Cresta Run at St Moritz. 'I think it's because I have so much to lose that I tempt the fates,' he told friends who expressed concern at his insatiable passion for danger.

In the early summer months of 1966, Gunther returned to St Tropez where he had run with a team of affluent cronies for almost a decade. He knew, of course, it was also Bardot's territory and that she, too, headed her own team. They had never met. For the most part, Bardot preferred to remain inside the high whitewashed walls of her villa, La Madrague, sunbathing, swimming nude, unseen by the outside world, surrounded by a few handpicked friends of both sexes, and her inevitable pride of pets of all kinds. The commercial natives of St Tropez owe a lot of their rich summer pickings to the omnipresence of Brigitte Bardot; her introspective occupation is felt, they say, throughout the small florescent town. 'She is the spirit of St Tropez,' says a café proprietor. 'She is the queen inside the palace. That is enough.'

One night, the queen left the palace to dine at a waterfront restaurant. She was escorted by several houseguests and her current lover, a handsome Brazilian promoter named Bob Zaguri. At a nearby table was Roger Vadim, dining with Gunther Sachs. Vadim introduced them. Bardot was naturally interested in Gunther Sachs as all women are in men with wicked reputations and cash to ride the carousel. She saw a man with eyes you remember, dark and watchful, not without humour. They were set deep in the sort of face that has eliminated childhood from its history. A handsome face but without atmosphere, somehow without secrets and shadows: built with almost aesthetic Bauhaus functionalism, it was a piece of modern furniture of a face. Mostly Brigitte noted his voice. Women have said it is the most charming thing about him. There is no single accent in his tone.

There is German, of course, but it is Gallicised now, just as his English is the transatlantic kind spoken by people in the movie business.

It was a brief, pleasant, polite encounter. A cautious summing-up testing first round. 'You seem to have been avoiding me for ten years,' Gunther told her, aware of the provocation in his voice. 'I hadn't noticed,' Brigitte replied.

The following morning, the stylish Saxy – as Brigitte was soon calling him, succumbing to her old weakness for nicknames – sent her one hundred red roses. Such richly attentive behaviour impressed Brigitte, a woman apt to judge the value of money not by quantity but by the use to which it is put. The style in which Gunther wooed Brigitte during the next seven days must have deeply satisfied his lust for speed . . . and the accompanying risk. At the Monte Carlo casino he gambled dashingly, winning some $75,000 and installing the whole party at the Hotel de Paris. He was infinitely more original, Brigitte privately acknowledged, than the actors, artists, and assorted St Tropez cowboys and consorts of late.

Confident of his crusading charm, Gunther lost no time in suggesting they fly to his Bavarian chalet for a rest. She accepted.

There was a certain Ruritanian splendour, a kind of Ivor Novello whimsy, about the events of the next seven days, best expressed by the violinists and guitar-players Gunther hired each evening to serenade beneath Brigitte's beflowered balcony. Brigitte was more than impressed. She wrote to Olga Horstig Primuz that she was 'truly truly in love for the first time' in her life. (How many times have you been in love? I asked her once. She said, 'A lot of times. But sometimes maybe it is better to tell myself I am in love and be happy than to think I am not in love and be sad!')

Without understanding the real scale of Gunther's life-style,

Brigitte accepted his proposal of marriage willingly. When a girlfriend later asked her why she thought it necessary to actually marry Gunther, she said: 'What else can you give a man who has everything? It was the most beautiful gift I could offer him at the time, I suppose!'

The couple, taking Roger Vadim's advice, flew to Las Vegas where marriages are obtainable without too much legal paraphernalia. The press caught up with them on the tarmac of the Los Angeles International Airport en route to Nevada. There they officially announced their very short engagement. A few hours later, shortly after midnight on 14th July – Bastille Day – 1966 they were married. (Senator Edward Kennedy, an old friend of Sachs, arranged the private jet aircraft which carried them on the final leg to Vegas. It was no doubt a welcome change: unable to get first-class accommodation at short notice, the couple – plus a photographer who went along to cover the elopement, wedding and honeymoon in Tahiti – had made the ten-hour flight to Los Angeles travelling tourist class.) The eight-minute ceremony, the vows made in English, was conducted in the sitting room of a local attorney by Judge John Mowbray who had been roused from his bed for the occasion.

Brigitte carried a single red rose – a sentimental memento of Gunther's first overture – and wore a thin silk purple shift. Gunther wore a white silk shirt open to the navel, black mohair blazer, white flannel slacks, moccasins, and no socks. (This final sartorial refinement, deplored several ladies in his punctilious past, was a distressing sign of the kind of influence Brigitte was already exerting. Brigitte denied it all. 'Gunther simply didn't have time to put his socks on,' she explained, the old glint of defiant concupiscence in her eyes.)

'May the road rise to meet you and may the wind be ever at your back,' toasted the judge in Dom Perignon champagne.

Brigitte wept.

In St Tropez, *les copains* were stunned, unable to take in the news from Las Vegas. 'She didn't mention any wedding plans to me,' said Bob Zaguri as he prepared to leave La Madrague. 'I thought she was shopping in Paris.'

The Dinner Circus

CHAPTER 10

THE SPEED WITH which Brigitte Bardot wed Gunther Sachs was bound to create certain problems. She soon discovered she hardly knew the man at all; she had married the image. The inabstinent courtship had the giddy compulsion of a high-class package tour: in a matter of weeks they had gone from strangers in St Tropez to man and wife in Las Vegas – taking in the pleasures of Monte Carlo, Bavaria, Paris and Los Angeles along the way. Gunther even found time to buy her a pet cheetah, Princesse – 'to celebrate my love of speed and your love of wild things,' he told her.

Brigitte had never been courted with such inspiration. 'He charters private jet planes,' she told a friend, 'the way most people call a taxi.' Somewhat thrifty herself, she could not help but admire his expensive wild whims, such as arranging a dinner party in a favourite Marbella restaurant for that evening – while still lunching in Paris. But a man's image, like a woman's mirror, has no soul. It was not only Gunther's volatile eating habits that Brigitte found indigestible, finally.

Her husband's apartment on the Avenue Foch in Paris was, for her, a home in an iron lung. 'It has no warmth, no real life,' she lamented aloud. 'It frightens me.' It was typical of those very expensive elegant barren homes put together by trendy decorators, a home full of textbook taste and imitation personality.

'Brigitte was appalled,' recalls a girl friend. 'She discovered all the beautiful books were just part of the set-dressing, just empty leather spines bought by the yard.' She named the apartment the Gunther Hilton. 'I really can't live with that,' she announced firmly.

The threatened dilemma was resolved very simply, as it happened. Gunther somehow omitted to give her a key, an oversight that in the circumstances didn't unduly disturb his bride. She continued to reside, for the most part, in her own apartment on the Avenue Paul Doumer.

But her friends became uneasy after a while. She was beginning to appreciate too well, explained one former lover, the cynical wisdom of Chekhov's advice: 'If you are afraid of loneliness, don't marry.' The fear of loneliness has troubled Bardot all her life. 'I hate to be alone. I get very anxious when I'm alone. Solitude scares me. It makes me think very strangely. I get anxious about life and death and war . . . I don't want to think so much,' she once told me. 'That is why I am always with good friends. I need distractions from the anxious thoughts, the black thoughts.'

Still, in his bizarre boy-next-door fashion, Gunther was trying to make her happy. 'He embarked on a campaign to convince her it was possible to live relatively well on a great deal of money,' says one wry observer of that scene. Many of Bardot's wisest friends believed he would win. 'Gunther is going to be good for Brigitte,' insisted Roger Vadim, whose hand in the affair had not been unnoticeable. 'Gunther is strong, a real man. She needs that.'

Brigitte appeared in the beginning to be going along with the Gunther game, accepting grand dinner dates, returning hospitality with lavish suppers at their various homes. 'Gunther always wanted dozens of people around them, there would be twenty people to dinner when Brigitte thought they were going to dine alone. It was a circus. Brigitte was more alone in those anonymous Sachs smart-set crowds than she's ever been in her life. She was literally losing her husband in the mob.'

Gunther's detractors insist he never intended the marriage to be more than an extension of his image. If a playboy's status is relative to the fame or notoriety of his wife or mistress, as one French writer contends, then clearly Gunther Sachs had bounded to the very top of the heap. It seemed to be a state of affairs that satisfied him rather well. 'He would invite a hundred-and-fifty people to dinner at Maxim's simply to show off Brigitte. It was all so alien to everything she had worked for,' claims one of the star's life-long friends.

Certainly, until the arrival of Gunther, Brigitte had managed to close down her social life to almost hermitical proportions by film star standards. When not working, she lived mostly within the walls of La Madrague, or on her remote and rambling farm near Bazoches forty-five miles outside Paris, going barefoot, in jeans, listening to records (including interminable Bach), reading, playing the guitar, swimming, fussing over her pets for hours. Even the most intimate houseguests – and she was never without someone close by she could completely rely on – couldn't be sure of their welcome from day to day, even from hour to hour.

'You were used as a kind of background dressing. You felt somehow you were important to her well-being, but she could completely ignore you for days on end,' says a minor actress who belonged, briefly, to Bardot's inner circle a few seasons ago.

'Brigitte's real trouble,' suggests Vadim, 'is that she doesn't really like people. She is like a selfish child living in a nursery world of her own creation. She cannot accept she is part of a larger society.'

A Paris designer who has known Brigitte since 1948, the year she first modelled for the fashion magazine *Jardin des Modes* says:

'She still has the same dewy-eyed ingenuousness. Only now she has lost touch with reality at crucial points. It makes her a disconcerting and difficult friend to have.'

The interpretations are myriad and some are too extravagant to be considered at all. Her long-time agent and friend, Mme Primuz cuts through a lot of the fantasy and mush and says: 'She wants to live simply, well, and on her own terms. She is like a wild animal a little bit, you know. She feels as if she is in jail if she has made a dinner date for a week ahead: she hates to plan the future.'

But Gunther Sachs was a planner, an organiser, and a natural publicist. 'He is a born tour leader,' Brigitte sighed. 'He refuses to follow me even a little way into my world.' Slowly but surely even his expensive gifts – including a white Rolls Royce complete with black liveried chauffeur – failed to impress her. 'I would much prefer a key ring chosen with love,' she told an English reporter just a hundred days after their Las Vegas elopement. 'Our tastes are so different. He loves everything luxurious, loud, and he loves photographers and publicity.'

Brigitte knew the marriage was doomed. But there was a lot more behind that extraordinarily revealing outburst than was at first apparent. 'I think that money often removes a lot of the humanity from a man,' she told me when Gunther had finally gone. 'When a man can buy anything he wants, when he can buy a girl because she is beautiful, when he can seduce her with jewellery, usually something nice dies in the spirit.'

There can be little doubt that such reflections are autobiographically inspired. Certainly those around her in that difficult autumn of 1966 knew all about the self-doubts tormenting her. There is a definite puritan streak in Bardot somewhere, a remnant seam of embedded childhood catholicism perhaps. She suspected she had somehow allowed herself to be bought by Gunther's impulsive but essential generosity. (Did something nice die in the victim's spirit, too?)

'I suspect she felt embarrassed, perhaps even a little humiliated, for the first time in her life,' said an English actor close to the stress of '66. 'She was obviously very mixed-up but she genuinely believed that her own strict private moral code had been abused. And from the moment she started thinking on those lines, Gunther Sachs didn't stand a chance.' Money, she had discovered at least, had no aphrodisiacal effect on her at all.

Brigitte may also have been quietly brooding over a vehement new attack on her by the church. A Dominican priest, in an open letter published in the weekly magazine *Vie Catholique Illustre,* said: 'In eight minutes you got married again in Las Vegas. You no longer belong to M Vadim, nor to M Charrier, nor to M Zaguri: you belong to M Sachs. In eight minutes you swear faithfulness for life. If someone else comes on the scene tomorrow whom you do not know today, will you get married again? Will M Sachs in turn use the words attributed to your last boy friend, M Zaguri, when he heard about your recent marriage – that it is all a big joke?'

This letter, coming when it did, troubled Bardot more deeply than she cared to admit. Publicly she said only this, 'Some people seem to prefer it only when I stick with lovers.'

Images of Instant Mesalliance . . .

CHAPTER 11

ON 2ND SEPTEMBER 1966, some seven weeks after the Las Vegas adventure, Brigitte Bardot flew to Scotland to begin work on her thirty-fourth film and the first Anglo-French production ever attempted. *Two Weeks in September* (seventy per cent French; thirty per cent English) was clearly going to be a movie fraught with partisanship as well as the usual front office and artistic tensions. Moreover, Brigitte was under a personal blight. She was beginning a film for the first time in her career without a lover or husband beside her, a man to constantly reassure her and console her in time of need. Gunther to her astonishment had elected to go shooting (a sport she thoroughly despised) in Germany.

Kenneth Harper, the British producer on the project, had misgivings from the beginning. The French contingent did nothing to disguise their *amor patriæ*. The English version (each scene had to be shot in two languages) was regarded with considerable casualness, even disdain. Bardot dislikes acting in English even now, and does so with voluble discomfort. The French director Serge Bourguignon had recently returned from Hollywood where he had made his first English-speaking film, *The Reward*. It had been an unmitigated flop and he was naturally less than confident about embarking on another movie in the English language. The Anglo–French agreement, he told Harper, was merely a financial convenience and had nothing whatsoever to do with creative thinking. English dialogue could simply be dubbed onto the French version later, he reasoned.

'It's going to be a bumpy ride,' Harper told the National Film Finance Corporation which had money in the movie. 'It was,' he ruefully admits now, 'rather worse than that.'

A few weeks before shooting began, Bourguignon, a handsome Napoleonic figure with a lot of theatrical charm, assured Harper that, whatever else, he could 'control Bardot completely'. He boasted, 'There is nothing she won't do for me'. It is naturally reassuring to know that your director is able to handle a leading lady of such valiant temperament; Harper was pleased to hear that Bourguignon was at least confident on that score.

But even that shred of serenity was short-lived. 'A week or so later, Bourguignon was boasting to me about the marvellous time he'd had riding down to the South of France with Bardot. I knew then he'd blown it skyhigh. It was a classic mistake. And it showed. She had no respect for him at all after that,' says Harper.

The arrival of Michael Sarne on the set was the distraction Brigitte had been waiting for. Gunther Sachs had come, played a few fitful rounds of golf, and gone. Bardot had reached the finger-drumming stage, a condition that appeared to tax director Bourguignon's confidence considerably.

Sarne, a former British pop star, had an aggressive sexuality Bardot clearly found interesting. He had the pale emaciated good-looks, the sunken temples and excavated cheeks, of an aesthetic lifer. He was intelligent, ambitious, and highly articulate. He possessed that sharp duality of narcissism and self-ridicule, not unusual in educated pop celebrities. His defamers said he was too full of himself, too cocky by half, to know how to behave with women. But he must have been doing something right.

Bardot, of course, was now accustomed to having an entourage ready to chorus *bravo* everytime she stirred her tea. She was amused by Michael Sarne's studied indifference. It wasn't a new line (it was a very old line as a matter of fact) but Sarne – a few years younger, infinitely poorer, with a vulnerably minor role in the film – played it well. He had just enough humour to soften the impudence and enough assurance to keep the electricity coming. Most American girls and a lot of English ones would have quit right there. Bardot deliberately took the bait.

'She took a shine to Mike and they went underground for a few days. We had a bit of a job prising them out, actually,' recalls Kenneth Harper with a repaired nonchalance that was badly bashed about in that autumn collision in 1966.

But an affair is more difficult to mount than an indiscretion, even such a protracted indiscretion. Sarne soon discovered that protocol as well as passion was going to be necessary if their relationship was to survive the production which had now shifted back to the Billancourt studios, Paris.

'When Brigitte Bardot and I met, it was on neutral territory. Let's call it Yalta,' says Sarne. 'A film set. We reached an *entente cordiale*. She then withdrew to her territory: Paris, the South of France, her own ballpark. It was not my ballpark. I was a stranger there, and consequently at considerable disadvantage. My territory is London, New York. I know what I'm doing in those towns.'

Sarne respected the mind he was dealing with. 'Bardot is not a flighty little girl. The girl is irresistible because she has made a careful study of being irresistible for nearly forty years. Every day she thinks about money, power, furthering the image, being happy, getting the upper hand. She worries about these things all day long. She worries so much that she sometimes breaks out in a rash.'

After some arbitration, some diplomacy, Bardot agreed to fly to London. 'She came to the flat I shared with Michael Chow (the Chinese restaurateur) in the Chiswick High Road.'

Brigitte Bardot and Chiswick High Road W4 are images of instant mesalliance, alas. Sarne could see it at once. 'She stayed a while but we both knew she did not belong there. It was impossible for her to survive in that alien atmosphere.' Neither side was prepared to make concessions. Says Sarne, 'If a guy can keep making her happy and believing in the romance, keep going along with the trips she wants to make . . . then she'll keep him around. Once he starts trying to haul her on to his trip, the writing's on the wall. He becomes a business associate, a chauffeur, the tame producer. He is no longer the lover because Bardot knows he can use sex as a way of controlling her.'

So they parted. Goodbye, Bébé, and Amen. It was an interlude some men dream about. 'I had more fun and more excitement with Brigitte Bardot in the short time I knew her than with any other woman I have ever known,' says Sarne. 'Any young boy's going to have his head turned, isn't he? Bardot was a . . . legend!'

He has come a long way since achieving the remarkable feat of taking a legend down to the High Street. The director of *Johanna* (with the extraordinary Genevieve Waite) and *Myra Breckinridge* (with Mae West and Raquel Welch) Michael Sarne must now be regarded as something of an expert on sex symbols, ancient and modern. His views on the subject are quite original.

'Mae West never had children; Brigitte has a son but she isn't a real mother. Both women have deliberately and cold-bloodedly renounced motherhood to sustain the pleasures of their youth when every man in the world wanted to make love to them,' he says. 'They both know that at the age of seventeen they made it all work beautifully; they dare not mess about with the formula. They don't want to try a new level of experience – like motherhood – if it threatens the pleasures and profits they get from being movie stars. Mae and Brigitte have inordinate respect for women with children and husbands and nice neat homes in the suburbs of life. They admire normal women who have taken the moral route through life, made sacrifices they themselves haven't made: the fact is, of course, Mae and Brigitte have made all the sacrifices.'

The heavy price of legend can be guessed at. Both women dote on their surrogate children. Admits Sarne in a poignant after-thought: 'Mae has her monkies, diapered and mooned over; Brigitte has her collection of animals, fondled and caressed like real human infants.'

But it is, on the whole, a hard-eyed professional opinion, delivered not without affection and a kind of compassion too. Perhaps Brigitte Bardot recognises the desolating validity of it all: perhaps she did long ago teach herself to discard such thoughts. (Nicholas, her son, is now thirteen years old. He lives with his father Jacques Charrier and his stepmother. He seldom sees his real mother. 'I don't want him to be confused by seeing me too often,' Brigitte explains. 'I don't want him to have worries about . . . where is my family? where is my home?' I once asked whether she was ever disturbed when she saw him. 'Not at all,' she said. 'Only . . . surprised!')

'She doesn't love children,' insists Roger Vadim. 'She is too much of a child herself. To her a child is a competitor. Not a simple competitor between her and a husband but a competitor for attention. A baby, a small child, needs attention constantly – just like Brigitte. She couldn't stand that. Maybe she will change one day but I never regret not having a child with Brigitte.'

Brigitte Bardot, argues Sarne, has paranoia: 'But paranoia and panic of that order clearly create fantastic results. If you said to Bardot: "You must abandon your fame but you can have real happiness with a brood of kids" she would laugh in your face.

She has genuinely convinced herself that what she's losing as a woman isn't worth as much as she gains as a legend.'

If Michael Sarne is right about the workings of myth, is it all really worth it?

'What would you say to Napoleon on Elba? You climb into a boat, row over to the island and say, "Okay, Bonaparte, was it all worth it?" I mean, it's balls, isn't it? How dare we ask Mae West and Brigitte Bardot that kind of question.'

A Girl to 'Ignite with Sean'

CHAPTER 12

AT ALMOST THE same time as Brigitte Bardot was flying to Scotland for the start of *Two Weeks in September*, a young British producer named Euan Lloyd was on his way to the Venice Film Festival to hustle finance for a low-budget western he wanted to make in Spain. He carried letters of agreement with Henry Fonda and Viennese actress Senta Berger to star, and Edward Dymytrik to direct. It wasn't a bad package; it wasn't fantastic either. Fonda, a fine solid veteran with a shrewd sense of his own middle-aged charisma, had warned Lloyd: 'I don't think you'll raise much money on my name these days. If you have any trouble, forget about me and get a name you can sell. Don't let it bother you. We'll do something else together some day.' Unfortunately, Henry Fonda read the situation accurately. The dealers at Venice liked the script but complained it was underpowered in the casting department. Lloyd returned to London without a deal.

Then he had an idea that has occurred to a lot of desperate promoters down the years, with varying degrees of success and disaster. He would go for broke! If he couldn't get his western off the ground as a low-budget production, he would make it as expensive as he knew how.

About that time, Sean Connery had announced his first

retirement from the James Bond role; he was between pictures, directing a documentary on the Glasgow shipyards. The script was immediately dispatched to him. (Connery's price at that time was somewhat more than the picture's original budget of one million dollars.) 'There were weeks and weeks of agony,' recalls Lloyd. 'Connery refused to make a decision until he'd finished his documentary.' Back in London at last, Connery said yes.

But Sean Connery and Senta Berger wasn't the right chemistry at all. 'Senta is a lovely lady but she and Sean didn't make the sparks fly. I had to find a girl who would ignite with Sean when you put them together on the screen.'

Euan Lloyd tramped the length and breadth of Hyde Park, a favourite thinking ground of his. When he finally hit on the idea of Brigitte Bardot, he remembers, 'My publicist's hat went up in the air, but my producer's hat stayed firmly on my head.' The chemistry was perfect, but . . . My instinct warned me to be careful. Bardot is one of the most exciting women God ever put on film but she doesn't necessarily sell tickets.' The indecision drove him around Hyde Park a few more times. 'If she creates that kind of excitement, that kind of stir, there has to be a reason why she's not selling tickets,' he reasoned. 'She has to be making the wrong pictures.'

The producer put in a call to Bardot's agent in Paris. 'Olga, a general question. No commitments, nothing at all. I can't even tell you what I'm thinking. But I want to know whether Brigitte is available from 1st January until sometime in May next year?'

Mme Primuz confirmed that she was. It was nearly midnight. Lloyd called Connery but he was out. He left a message for the actor to call the moment he got in. 'I'd been warned by the agent that there was something else in the wind but that's the oldest story in the world but still I wasn't taking any risks.' At 3 am

Connery returned his call, somewhat ruffled by the late hour. 'What's so desperate that you have to talk to me in the middle of the night?' he wanted to know.

'I'm going to say two words to you, then you can go to bed'. 'Brigitte Bardot!' said Lloyd.

'Bloody marvellous!' said Connery replacing the receiver.

The script was on the first plane to Paris that morning.

Brigitte Bardot liked the script and summoned Euan Lloyd to St Tropez for a weekend to discuss 'certain conditions.' The money question ($350,000 – fifty per cent up front, the rest over three years – plus fifteen per cent of the net profits) had already been settled with Mme Primuz in Paris. The contract, however, had still not been signed and if the producer showed a little edginess that weekend it was understandable.

Producer Harry Saltzman had arrived in town. He was trying to nail Bardot for his next James Bond movie. 'He'd heard I was after her for the Connery western,' says Lloyd. 'He obviously figured if he couldn't have Connery for *On His Majesty's Secret Service*, he'd steal his leading lady from under his nose.' (There was a lot of needle between Saltzman and Connery at that time.)

With Harry Saltzman ensconced at the Byblos and breathing down his neck, Lloyd was naturally anxious to sew up his deal with Bardot as fast as he possibly could. 'I have one condition.' Bardot fortunately came straight to the point. 'I have to meet Mr Connery before I will sign for your picture.'

'I thought: Jesus Christ!' remembers Lloyd. Connery had returned to Glasgow to complete his shipyard documentary; Lloyd knew he wouldn't be available for at least two weeks. But timing was suddenly the least of the producer's troubles: 'How do you tell Sean Connery that he's on approval?'

Lloyd decided to play it perfectly straight. 'She'll do the picture but she wants to meet you first.' he told the actor.

'Well,' said Connery, locking himself into a long unnerving silence, 'where?'

Lloyd had that answer figured out. It had to be close to a good golf course to please Connery. It had to be somewhere in France to please Bardot. It had to be in a neutral setting to reassure both of them. The producer believed he had the difficult ego equation exactly right.

'Deauville,' he said.

There was a flicker of resentment in Connery's eyes: 'If she thinks I'm going over to France to be given the once over she can fucking well forget it,' he flared up.

'It's nothing like that Sean,' Lloyd assured him quickly. It was a critical moment. 'She simply wants to see if you can work together. After all, you're going to be pretty close for twelve weeks. She's just anxious to make sure you're *sympatico* together. She's dying to meet you.' Connery relaxed. 'Okay,' he said. 'Fix it.'

The summit meeting in Deauville was a remarkable success. 'They looked at each other and you knew what she was thinking and you knew what he was thinking. You could have cut it with a knife. Bingo! That was it,' recalls Lloyd, the awe of it all still in his voice as if it were yesterday.

Gunther Sachs, still in some connubial contact with his wife, and never one to miss an occasion to celebrate, threw a fancy dress dinner party for fifty close friends who happened to be in Deauville at the time. That evening, Bardot told the producer: 'Oh by the way, I will make your picture.'

'What really happened in Deauville,' admits Lloyd, 'I don't know. They were clearly in some sort of communion, and feeling

great together. They were like two peas in a pod. Just write your
own cliche.'

Shalako, set in New Mexico in the 1880's, began filming in
Almeria, Southern Spain, in the middle of January 1968. On the
first morning Brigitte Bardot (in her white Rolls Royce driven
by the ubiquitous, photogenic black chauffeur) arrived at the
head of a cavalcade of forty-seven motorcars, each carrying one or
more press photographer. *Shalako* had come a long way from the
low-budget proposition Euan Lloyd had taken to Venice in 1966.

Sean Connery watched the extraordinary entrance with steely
eyes. 'Somebody,' he finally told publicity chief Kenneth Green
evenly, 'has to tell this lady that this is going to be a serious film.
Not a bloody circus.'

It was a tricky situation for Green, the man who had helped
Bardot when she first arrived in London back in 1956. A publicity
man's job is to make as widely known as possible the existence
of his producer's product. And Brigitte Bardot, Green recalls
with affectionless admiration, 'was the publicity man's dream.'
Publicity must be controlled and often manipulated, but to ask a
publicist to dissuade a phenomenon like Bardot is like asking
Niagara Falls not to splash.

Bardot slid into a repertoire of poses with such mechanical
ease that Green half expected to find a key plunged between her
shoulder blades. When photographers are around there is no
mobility in her beauty at all: each smile, frown, laugh, pout and
scowl seems to be projected onto her face in single frames to be
captured at 1/1,000 of a second and processed for posterity. 'We
were getting ten, twelve, fifteen photographers a day, from every
corner of the globe. She would go through a series of poses each
hour of the day,' says Green. 'She would comb her hair, fix her
lipstick, light a cigaratte, lift up her skirt and pretend to be fixing
her shoe. She would even go and pat the horses – although she

hates horses. She had this incredibly acute sense of what newspapers and magazines wanted.'

Whatever the taciturn Scot Sean Connery felt about these antics it didn't trouble producer Euan Lloyd too seriously. He was getting his money's worth. 'I was fairly blunt to myself about Bardot,' he says now. 'I knew that she had fairly limited box-office appeal – but fantastic publicity appeal. I was spending $350,000 on her as an actress in the picture. I actually believed she was very good for the role. But a woman in any western has a very limited part to play. I was really buying several million dollars worth of publicity. I make no apologies for it.'

Gunther Sachs, meanwhile, had visited Almeria and declared the town 'ugly, dirty and too hot' and after three days returned to Paris. If Gunther was beginning to see red, it is understandable. It was the colour Brigitte had decided to paint the town.

'She suddenly seemed to become obsessed with the idea of proving that she was ageless, a perennial teenager who wanted to show that she could go on dancing, singing and whooping it up all night, ' says Kenneth Green.

The Dying of a Dog

CHAPTER 13

'IT SEEMED,' SAYS Euan Lloyd now, 'like a very good idea at the time.'

Shortly before Brigitte Bardot arrived at the Hotel Aguatulce, where she was to stay during the making of *Shalako*, he had installed an expensive stereo system throughout her suite on the top floor. No money was spared on the operation; speakers were fitted into every room, including the several bathrooms. 'I knew she adored music and I wanted her to be happy during her stay,' he explained.

Unfortunately, the Aguatulce (built quickly to accommodate film companies who find local topography convenient for westerns) is a modern hotel with modern faults. One, soon to be uncovered, lay in the plumbing system.

If plugs were left out of baths or basins while music was being played in that room, the plumbing became an aquatical Tannoy system, carrying the sound throughout the entire building. Miss Bardot's penchant for fortissimo rhythms at 2 am soon became a talking point at the Agualtulce, especially by those who had to be up at 6 am to go to work. (The actress – who regarded the musical plumbing as a colossal jape and could not mention it without falling about in hysterics – was fortunate enough to have a clause in her contract stipulating that she did not have to be on the set before 10 am. 'I went along with that,' says Lloyd. 'What woman looks good before 10 am? Her face is her business.')

If Brigitte Bardot's face wasn't open for business too early, it certainly didn't seem to mind what time it shut up shop at night. 'She would throw parties for all kinds of people,' says Lloyd. 'Waiters from local restaurants, the rich, the poor, other actors, technicians. She had no fixed rules about whom she befriended. If a shoeshine boy had something she liked, he was her friend.'

The frenetic pace Bardot set in Almeria – a town she detested in a country she loathed – worried her friends. 'She was acting up like she had reached the last gas station before the desert,' said an American visitor. Some suspected she was heading for another and perhaps more serious crack-up. Her nerves were strung out like piano wires. 'The smallest incident was enough to set her off,' recalls a character actor on that location. 'She was practically a ledge-case.'

'There was,' instances Kenneth Green, 'the celebrated dog incident, of course. That says everything you want to know about the lady at that time.' On the way to the location one morning, Brigitte saw a pack of stray dogs, scavenging for food in a rubbish tip outside a small village. Moved by their bony plight, she immediately collected a large parcel of scraps from the location cookhouse and returned (in her white Rolls Royce with black chauffeur) to feed the dogs herself. One dog, however, caught her fancy. Against considerable advice and argument, Brigitte insisted that the animal be taken back to the hotel for her.

'Exhaustive inquiries were made,' says Green. 'Unfortunately, nobody could be found willing to lay claim to the animal.' The dog, showing signs of some surprise, even alarm, was duly picked up and taken back to the Aguatulce to become further acquainted with its bountiful new mistress. Bathed, perfumed, brushed and fed on plates of paté and other delicacies from Bardot's cupboard, the dog died in three days.

'It was inevitable. Until that point the animal had been living on rats, dead fish and anything it could steal,' says Green. 'It didn't stand a chance with all that French cuisine.' The studio labourer, handling the funeral arrangements, tried to console the actress: 'The poor little bleeder,' he is reputed to have assured her, 'looks a lot healthier dead than it ever did alive.'

Bardot was desolate. 'She could neither eat nor drink, nor talk nor work. Next to her own child and herself, that mangy mongrel was probably the only thing in this world she'd ever really loved. And she felt she'd let it down,' thinks Green.

For several hours on the day the dog died, Bardot sat in the executive dining tent while various members of her considerable entourage attempted to feed her with soup and coffee. 'Nothing,' says Green, 'could bring the smile back to this girl's face. She was actually . . . bereaved. It was a personal tragedy.' When Sean Connery sat beside her, a Frenchman sitting next to the English actor Jack Hawkins asked nervously, 'What is Connery going to say to her? He must be careful what he says!' 'Don't worry,' said Hawkins, using a suitably sepulchral tone. 'He is only conveying the condolences of Her Majesty the Queen.'

It was clear that Bardot was in no state to work that day. She was sent back to the hotel. 'There was no piped music that night,' remembers Euan Lloyd.

It is now reasonable to suppose that her grief over the dog was mostly an emotional enema to relieve other tensions. Her third marriage – the 'beautiful adventure' begun in Las Vegas, the gambling capital of the world – was clearly coming apart at the vows. Pictures began to appear in the papers of Gunther Sachs escorting beautiful women around the fun centres of Europe. 'In America,' recalls one of the fascinated crew, 'the Bardot merry-go-round just got faster and madder.' Her name was being linked with assorted young men around the place.

'Because she is what she is,' says Euan Lloyd, 'an extraordinary sex symbol who can pick and choose as no other woman in the world can, a great many very attractive males appear to hover in her vicinity hoping to be plucked . . . and, of course, it happens, because she does love attractive men.'

On the French radio at this time, Brigitte was quoted saying: 'It is better to be unfaithful than faithful without wanting to be. I can abandon someone whom I have loved. Nobody has any security in loving me. The problem is to hold on to me. That is difficult.'

It appeared to be a loaded innuendo pointing pretty obviously at Gunther. But her moods would shift swiftly and inexplicably. And when a rekindled friendship with actor Stephen Boyd – they first met back in 1957 in a piece of Vadim erotica called *Heaven Fell That Night* – leaked into the press she was furious.

'She accused us of engineering the whole thing as a publicity stunt,' says Green. 'Boyd, poor man, was upset and embarrassed. It was quite obvious that they had a very close personal friendship going, but certainly one would never feel it was of a very serious nature.' Having watched Brigitte's uninhibited behaviour in Almeria for weeks, Green was astonished and perplexed by her sudden indignation over the Boyd headlines. 'I have never seen an actress so angry,' he says. 'It became necessary to issue a calming statement; she was given four days off to go and sort out her problems.'

She flew straight to Sachs in St Moritz. Whatever they privately decided at that time, their marriage was to be kept at least legally alive for another eighteen months of rumour, denial, and inevitable scandal. They seldom met. 'I think,' said one of Gunther's cruder chums, 'he is phoning it in.'

Shalako was a success almost everywhere in the world. It was not a success in the United States, however, and it flopped in France, the only country in which Bardot got top billing over Connery. 'The point is,' says Euan Lloyd, 'I bet if you questioned anyone in this airport (we were lunching at Nice International Airport in the summer of 1972) they will have heard of a picture called *Shalako* – even if they have never seen it! Brigitte did everything that was asked of her. You finally forget about the difficulties and inconveniences, the late nights, the plumbed-in music, the fights over make-up (he felt she was overdoing her eye-shadow; she produced research and contemporary photographs to prove she wasn't: the critics still hated it) and all the personal dramas. She is a star worth accommodating. If it were a lot of so-called big-names today coming on that strong, I would have been less understanding perhaps. But Bardot . . . you give. She was absolutely fantastic. I adored her.'

But Bardot is nothing if not prismatic.

'In all my forty-three years in the film industry,' Kenneth Green reflected when the dust of *Shalako* had settled, 'I cannot remember an actress who was so arrogant, upstage, rude, and offhand. Except, of course, Bette Davis.'

Mister Lennon and The Maharishi Mazes

CHAPTER 14

UNLIKE KEATS, BRIGITTE Bardot's name is writ not in water but spilt milk. 'It is very hard to be happy in life for anybody,' she once told me as we contemplated her swell and troublous times. 'I suppose people with everyday worries – about money, children, bills, promotion – must think it is easy and lovely being a film star. But it isn't so easy, it isn't lovely at all as a matter of fact. Everybody can see you, everybody knows what you are doing, when you change lovers, when you have fights, if you have a spot on your nose.

'Stardom is a house without shades. And if you have no private life it is impossible to be really happy. There is a French proverb: *"To live happy, live hidden."* Where can Brigitte Bardot hide?' (In 1965, a Paris court ruled that she was entitled to privacy, with the right to refuse to be photographed when not working. She was awarded one franc symbolic damages against newspapers which ran unauthorised photographs of her, usually taken with prying telephoto lenses. The candid pictures did not stop appearing, however, as Gunther Sachs was soon obliged to observe to his lawyer.)

Trapped in the open space of public life, it sometimes seems that Bardot has decided simply to grow old disgracefully. Her outrageousness appears to have become both defiant and instinctive, a liability she can no longer discharge.

In a fracas with a lover, she fled through a window of her suite at the Monte-Real Hotel in Madrid, escaping into an adjoining apartment. The occupant, a middle-aged gentleman, awoke to find the world's greatest sex symbol at the foot of his bed. 'Pardon, m'sieur,' she whispered. 'Please don't bother to get up. I will let myself out.'

She was, the legend persists, quite naked at the time.

'Brigitte Bardot is the only star in the world capable of making man's most erotic dreams come true,' admires John Daly, British producer of the movie she was making at the time: *The Legend of Frenchie King*.

Shortly before her elopement with Gunther Sachs in 1966, Hal Shaper, the brilliant young South African lyricist was in Paris working on a proposed Bardot television special being prepared by the unsuspecting lover Bob Zaguri.

With Shaper was an English musical director who clearly found his proximity to the legendary sex goddess too exciting. 'He couldn't take his eyes off her,' recalls Shaper. 'She wore an incredibly short mini and her legs were perfectly tanned. I always thought that looking at her pins was pretty fancy myself. But this poor bloke was . . . obsessed! He followed her everywhere, his eyes glued to her legs. If she changed seats, he'd suddenly be sitting in the chair opposite her. It was getting just a little bit embarrassing, I must admit.'

The Englishman's reckless surveillance continued throughout most of the afternoon. Finally, Bardot walked across the room to within a foot of his flushed, excited face. She lifted her skirt amazingly high and said, 'If that is all you want to see, you might as well have a good look.'

' I thought,' remembers Shaper, 'he was going to die. Brigitte thought it was a great joke, of course. But it was too much for him. He returned to London the same evening and I was left without an MD. Finally it didn't make any difference, of course. The project was abandoned when Brigitte went off and married Gunther. It came as a hell of a shock to Bob Zaguri.'

Bardot's eclat, of course, grips her like a vice. Her instinctive tolerance of other people's behaviour, and a certain natural vanity about her own advertised freedoms, make her reluctant to rebuke even the most boorish guests. 'She has a quick sense of the ridiculous,' says an associate. 'It is a very useful safety valve for somebody so subjected to the most astonishing assumptions.' Take the strange encounter with John Lennon for instance.

'I'm Mr John Lennon's secretary,' said the man on the telephone. 'Mr Lennon sends his compliments and would like to call upon you while you are in London.' Admiring the inerrable and unexpected Victorian finesse of the approach, Bardot said at once that a meeting would be most agreeable to her.

The secretary then explained that Mr Lennon was at that time in something of an Eastern mood, was indeed much taken up with transcendental meditation, and would, when he arrived, prefer to repose on cushions. Moreover, any music played during his presence should also be of an Eastern flavour, preferably the sitar works of Ravi Shankar. It would, the secretary assured Bardot, enhance the happy vibrations that were already certain to exist between Bardot and the Beatle.

Solemnly agreeing it would be most inhospitable not to make Mr Lennon feel completely at home, Bardot arranged for all chairs and sofas to be removed from her suite at the Mayfair hotel. Every available cushion was thenceforth installed.

Shortly before the appointed hour of Lennon's curiously-heralded visit, the secretary arrived. He inspected the room, appreciated the cushions, and very seriously assured Bardot that the music was giving off the right vibrations. Finding everything in order, he left to fetch Mr Lennon who was outside in his Rolls Royce, presumably awaiting a favourable report from his man.

The Beatle was a big disappointment to Bardot. Ignoring the mountains of cushions, he promptly squatted on the floor. For almost thirty minutes he continued to sit in an Indian holy man position, not uttering a sound.

'India appears to have made quite an impression on you,' Bardot ventured after a while, knowing of his recent trip and hoping, naturally enough, to terminate his fascinating but socially-trying introspection.

'Don't ask questions,' Lennon answered pertly. 'Listen to the sounds, feel the vibes.' A religious experience, he said closing his eyes, was imminent.

Bardot, however, was content with her agnosticism. ('I live outside religion,' she once told me. 'People lean on organised religion too much: they use God as an alibi: they are wicked and they confess and they feel good again until the next time. Maybe there is a God but where or how I don't know. So when things are going bad for me I don't feel I have the right to ask Him for any favours. I wouldn't like to rely on somebody I only half believed in.')

Lennon continued his interior journey through the Maharishi mazes towards some private simple solace clearly some distance from the modern luxuries of the Mayfair suite. After several hours of this unorthodox gathering, Bardot suggested they should go to dinner. Lennon did not wish to risk eating while a religious experience was so close. He elected to remain in the suite until Bardot returned. 'While you are gone,' he said, briefly interrupting his cerebric exertions, 'I will compose a song for you.'

With this sudden promise of a breakthrough, Bardot and her companions left for dinner at Parkes in Beauchamp Place; Tom Benson's original cuisine was given added spice with the prospect of hearing Lennon's song on their return.

Bardot takes up the story: 'When we got back to the hotel, Lennon was asleep on the floor, surrounded by masses of cushions and flowers and empty beer bottles. His secretary had passed out in my bed. The Indian music was blaring away.' The vibes, it must be said, were not very propitious.

Lennon nevertheless roused himself sufficiently to attempt to render the promised anthem. It was not a memorable composition and he went back to sleep after only a few bars.

When Bardot checked out of the hotel the following morning, the management is alleged to have asked her never to come back again. 'Brigitte understood; there was no unpleasantness,' recalls a friend. 'You'd be surprised how often she has to pay the penalty for other people's behaviour.'

'When you read articles,' I started to ask her on one occasion, 'about the shocking Brigitte Bardot . . . '

'That is over now, no?' she rammed my question.

'Is it?'

'I hope not! But at a certain moment I was the first to be nude on the screen, the first to have the very hot love scenes. If I had been the second I would not be Brigitte Bardot. But now others have overtaken me. It's true. I started it . . . but now it is very ordinary to see the erotic and . . . well, so much!'

I asked her whether there were any scenes she would resist playing on the screen. 'It isn't that I'm shy,' she said. 'I will never become tame, I hope. But some acts are better performed in the boudoir without an audience.'

There is an endearing simplicity about Bardot, a gentleness and a sympathy that often touches her with a kind of absurd innocence. Nothing, for example, so pleases her as the contemplation of some animal yarn with a happy ending.

She may have difficulty establishing contact with children, indeed she appears to be able to dispense with them completely, but she has a hidden rapport with the old that is quite remarkable. 'There are a great many very old ladies she helps financially,' admits her agent, Mme Olga Horstig-Primuz. When Bardot changed apartments not long ago, she carefully saw to it that one neighbour, a woman past eighty, should also be moved to a nearby apartment.

'Whenever Brigite is away, wherever she is in the world, she will always call this woman,' says Mme Primuz. 'She may forget to call me about some business deal, she may not call her own mother, but she will be sure to telephone her old friend.'

Theoretically, says one French director, Brigitte has many friends: 'In practice she likes only the very old.' Says Mme Primuz, 'I think it is because the old are often helpless and need love like animals.'

The future has always scared Bardot. Her avoidance of fortune-tellers, clairvoyants and soothsayers of all kinds is almost paranoiac. But is her compulsive companionship with aged ladies her own way of coming to terms with the future? Not a few of her closest friends suspect it is.

'She is a little bit like a small child who is terrified of the dark but makes herself go into a graveyard at night,' suggests one actress who knows her well both professionally and privately. 'Brigitte will often sit with one old lady in Paris for hours on end – but all the time she is secretly weeping for Brigitte Bardot. In that old woman's face she can see the future clearer than any palmist can tell it.'

For all beautiful women, of course, the writing on the wall is first glimpsed between the lines of an old beauty's face. 'It fascinates her and frightens her, old age. If Brigitte doesn't learn before she reaches forty to accept that growing old is a universal destiny – then she might just kill herself, I think. It is her way.' It is a melancholy idea, but not so remarkable among those around Bardot today.

Anne Dussart, wife of Gicky Dussart, French painter, photographer and long-time friend of the star, says simply this: 'It will be a tragedy if Brigitte grows old because she doesn't understand growing old. Like a cat, like any wild thing, she doesn't comprehend the growing years, the movement of time, the passing days. She wants always to be young and do the things the young do.'

A Bare Removal—and a Plaster Cast

CHAPTER 15

BARDOT'S ESTRANGEMENT FROM Gunther Sachs did not go unnoticed. Her relationship with an Italian club owner named Luigi Rizzi was particularly evident. They were photographed together by the pool at La Madrague in various stages of sun worship. Sachs' statesmanlike silence on the matter was coming to an end. Still more indiscreet photographs appeared in an American magazine. Finally, as he was leaving Palma airport for Paris in August 1968, Sachs told an inquiring newsman: 'Look, if a man opens an international magazine and sees a picture of his wife naked, with a naked man, don't you think there are grounds for divorce!' (In private, after studying a picture of his undressed wife and her lover, Gunther more wryly remarked: 'I think the end is in sight, my friends.')

In September 1969 their marriage was officially ended in the Swiss town of Filisur, near St Moritz. There was no fuss; the press caught on to it a month later, but nobody was surprised. 'Now Brigitte is a three-time loser – official!', said a former lover, not sneering at all. 'Superficially,' Bardot told me later, 'Gunther was the man made to live with me. He was strong, rich and determined. But his life-style was so different from mine. It was finally impossible – so many footmen, butlers, maids. I hate domestic staff under my feet. I need only one.'

Some suspected she was looking for excuses.

'She can collect men with ridiculous ease,' said Michael Sarne. 'The tragedy is she can never resolve it. She never has and never will be able to follow through.'

But her legend has touched reality once too often. This time it was as if she had been watching herself perform in some sensory rear-view mirror, seeing the currents racing backwards: her childhood and her youth and the deserted Occupied streets of Passy and blank-faced lovers and antique applause and remote sorrows, and balked escape through open wrists.

It was the beginning of a new self-awareness in her, a real and tangible sense of dissatisfaction, a kind of spiritual anguish. 'At least as you get older,' she told a girl friend, 'you get the satisfaction of knowing yourself a little more. I'm beginning to understand a lot of things now.'

'It was,' the confidante wrote in her diary, 'the belated hindsight of a self-blinded voluptuary.' Adding, 'At last, at last.'

In Madrid in the summer of 1971 Bardot told me, 'I think I'm a better person than I was ten years ago. I do try to be better and better – without going to India! Without a guru! India is so crowded now, yes?' She laughed. Her face was luminous.

Beginnings, like the last embrace of a love affair, are often difficult to recognise when they are happening. But we had met, Bardot and I, several times, around the world, in Mexico and London, in Madrid, in Paris, and this time I had the feeling she was at the start of something. Something that was going to be interesting. There was about her that lazy satisfaction, a superior contentment of someone who has finally reached an important secret liberating decision.

On 28th September 1971, her thirty-seventh birthday, Brigitte Bardot left her home on the Avenue Paul Doumer, Paris, where she had lived for nearly fifteen years. She moved to a modern penthouse on Boulevard Lannes. She took almost nothing with her: no books, no paintings, no mementoes, no sentimental bric-a-brac. She put the apartment – lock, stock and barrel – on the market for $250,000.

'That place was suffocating me,' she said, dismissing it without a backward glance. 'So much happened to me there. There were too many memories. I could not breathe there. I did not want to be reminded of the past all the time, so much past.'

Her friends understood. 'Bumping into ghosts,' said one, 'can be very painful.'

At the end of 1971 I returned to Paris. Bardot invited me to the new apartment. She wore hot pants and a thin silk shirt and high suede boots. From less than ten feet she looked like a woman in her early twenties, no more. Closer she still looked like a million dollars, in used notes, but still a million dollars. The fine lines around the wide-apart eyes and mouth are like delicate autumn twigs silhouetted against evening sky. They remind you that she is a woman moulded by nature, before the silicon season spawned its flock of ornamental imitators.

She is wise enough now, Bardot, despite her fears of growing old, to let alone the peeling finery and melting glitter of old triumphs. Her make-up is light. It is hard to believe that twenty years have gone since she first sashayed into our lives, so nubile and naked and wired to shock. The dancer's grace is still in her walk. There is something more than atropine and lemon juice in her eyes to make them shine so well.

Strobe lights popped and twitched on the balcony high over the city; Bob Dylan sang on the record-player; a television set played to itself in a far corner of the L-shaped room, a log fire

141

coughed discreetly in the brand new canopied fireplace, too polite to spit. The exquisite pieces were a bit like the first guests to arrive at a party, not knowing each other, not sure of their place: there was a precise separateness about everything that created a sense of isolation that wasn't meant. The ambience squeaked like new shoes.

Even so, you could tell it was a new apartment – her new beginning – from the way she showed it off. We went from room to room, sipping our Scotch, she as quietly excited as a child close to Christmas, knowing where the toys are hidden.

All the time I was remembering conversations with Vadim. 'She exists mostly in the imagination of others now. She has become the true myth. In the sun she is without a shadow. You cannot reach out and hold her now . . . she is a night thought.'

In the drawing room, games of every kind spilled over the tables: miniature roulette wheels, dice, packs of cards, puzzles, checkers.

'Little by little,' said Vadim, 'there is nothing around her but emptiness. And she becomes herself more empty.' The bedroom is white and contains not much more than a television set and the bed: over the bed is a white plaster cast of a nude woman masturbating; on the bed her latest lover, Christian Kalt, a sometime ski-instructor and Riviera cowboy, watches a football game on television.

'She needs constant praise and love and admiration,' said Vadim, 'to reassure herself that she really does exist.'

When she was young, she told me once, she met Picasso. 'But it was too soon for me to understand, I was too young to appreciate his genius. I didn't ask him anything.'

'What would you ask him now?' I said.

'Do you love me, Picasso?' she answered.

Index

Allégret Marc, 22, 29, 43, 44
Anouilh Jean, 40
Axelrod George, 52

Baer Max, 11
Bardot Anne-Marie, 12–18, 30, 80
Bardot Louis, 12, 13, 32, 37
Bardot Mijanou, 30, 32
Barelli Aimé, 19
Barrate Jean, 20, 21
Belmondo Jean Paul, 29
Benson Tom, 133
Berger Senta, 113
Bogarde Dirk, 47–49
Bonnie and Clyde, 11
Bourget Madame, 14, 15
Bourguignon Serge, 105
Box Betty, 47, 48, 50
Boyd Stephen, 124
Breaud Francine, 74
Burton Richard, 81

Camus Albert, 19
Carnera Primo, 11

Chandler Raymond, 18
Chanel, 20, 48
Charrier Jacques, 75–82
Charrier Nicholas, 76, 109
Checkov, 98
Chow Michael, 108
Clair René, 52
Clouzot Henri, 78, 79
Cocteau Jean, 19
Connery Sean, 113–118
Coty, 20

Daily Herald, 68
Daly John, 130
Davies Jack, 48
Davis Bette, 125
de Beauvoir Simone, 65, 83
de Havilland Olivia, 43
Delamere Rosine, 20
Deneuve Catherine, 83
Dillinger John, 11
Disney Walt, 29
Distel Sacha, 73–75, 79
Doepfner Cardinal, 65
Duras Marguerite, 68

Durante Jimmy, 11
Dussart Anne, 135
Dussart Gicky, 135
Dylan Bob, 141
Dymytrik Edward, 113

Elle, 21, 22

Faure Anne-Marie, 88
Feuillere Edwige, 40
Fonda Henry, 113
Frey Sammy, 78, 79

Gabin Jean, 29, 67–68
Gillespie Dizzy, 19
Gordon Doctor Richard, 48
Gourdan-Aslan Alain, 65
Greco Juiliette, 19
Green Kenneth, 50, 117–125
Greene Graham, 81
Guerlain, 48

Harlow Jean, 11
Harper Kenneth, 105
Hawkins Coleman, 19
Hawkins Jack, 123
Hayworth Rita, 21
Huston John, 52
Inge William, 52

Jardin des Modes, 21, 99

Kalt Christian, 142
Keats John, 129
Kennedy Senator Edward, 92
Khan Ghengis, 22

Laaf Birgitta, 89
Lennon John, 131, 133
Levy Raoul, 28, 55–58, 63, 78
Litvak Anatole, 52
Lloyd Euan, 113–121, 123
Logan Joshua, 52
Luter Claude, 19

Mangano Sylvana, 40
Mistinquette, 19
Mitchum Robert, 52
Monro Marilyn, 52, 64, 67
Moreau Jeanne, 83
Mowbray Judge John, 92

Napoleon, 31
Novello Ivor, 91

Olivier Sir Lawrence
  (now Lord), 52
Onassis Tina, 89

Paris Match, 32, 38, 40
Picasso Pablo, 142
Phipps Nicholas, 48
Plemianikoff M, 27, 28
Plemianikoff Mme, 28

Poiret Paul, 20
Primuz Olga Horstig, 40, 66, 82, 69, 100, 114, 134

Rizzi Luigi, 139
Robbins Harold, 88
Rodgers and Hart, 11

Sachs Gunther, 87–105, 116–118, 123–130, 139
Sagon Francoise, 83
Saltzman Harry, 115
Sarne Michael, 106–112, 140
Sartre Jean-Paul, 19
Schiaperilli Elsa, 20
Shankar Ravi, 131
Shaper Hal, 130
Simenon Georges, 67
Simon Simone, 23
Soraya Princess, 89
Stavisky Serge, 12
Stroyberg Annette, 79

Teagarden Jack, 11
Thomas Ralph, 47–50, 66
Time magazine, 83
The Times, 11
Todd Mike, 55
Trintignant Jean Louis, 56, 60, 67–73, 78
Turner Lana, 43

Valentino Rudolph, 80
Vadim Roger, 22–63, 65–68, 75, 89, 98, 109
Versois Odile, 47
Vie Catholique Illustre, 101

Waite Genevieve, 108
Welch Raquel, 108
West Mae, 11, 108–110
Worth, 20
Wyman Jane, 21

Zaguri Bob, 90–93, 130, 131

A Filmography

BRIGITTE BARDOT

LE TROU NORMAND (The Norman Hole) 1952, France.
Eighty-five minutes.

Production: Cité-Film *Director:* Jean Boyer *Producer:* Jacques
Bar *Script & dialogue:* Arlette de Pitray *Photography:* Charles
Suin *Editor:* Fanchette Mazin *Art Director:* Robert Giordani
Music: Paul Misraki *Lyrics:* Jean Boyer *Sound:* William Sivel
Production manager: Walter Rupp *Assistant directors:* Jean Bastia
and Gilbert Guez *Shooting:* begun on 12th May 1952; exteriors
at Conches and environs *Première:* 7th November 1952, Paris
British release details: None *Leading players:* Bourvil (Hypolite),
Jane Marken (Augustine), Brigitte Bardot (Augustine's daughter),
Nadine Basile (the teacher), and Jeanne Fusier-Gir, Pierre Larquey,
Noël Roquevert, Georges Baconnet, Florence Michaël.

Story summary: Hypolite is to inherit a prosperous inn called
'Le Trou Normand' on condition that he gains a certificate of
education. So at the age of thirty-two, he begins scholastic
studies. His enterprise is not to the liking of aunt Augustine (with
whose daughter he is in love), who stands to inherit the inn if he
fails his examination. With the help of a young teacher, Hypolite
wins through.

MANINA, LA FILLE SANS VOILE (Manina, the Unveiled Girl) 1952, France. Issued in English as *The Lighthouse-keeper's Daughter*. Eighty-six minutes.

Production: Sport Films *Director:* Willy Rozier *Script:* Xavier Vallier *Adaptation & dialogue:* Willy Rozier *Photography:* Michel Rocca *Editor:* Suzanne Baron *Music:* Jean Yatove *Lyrics:* Xavier Vallier *Sound:* André Le Baut *Production manager:* René Jaspard *Assistant director:* Louis Pascal *Shooting:* begun on 30th June 1952; exteriors at Golfe Juan, Cannes, Nice, Paris, Bonifacio, Ile de Lavesi and Tangiers *British release details:* distributed by Gala Films, 1959, in a reduced version of fifty-seven mins, cert. 'U' *Leading players:* Brigitte Bardot (Manina), Jean-François Calvé (Gérard), Howard Vernon (Eric), and Espanita Cortez, Raymond Cordy, Robert Arnoux.

Story summary: Law student Gérard and smuggler Eric join forces in a successful attempt to locate a sunken Phoenician treasure ship off the Corsican coast. Gérard combines this activity with the wooing of the lighthouse-keeper's daughter, Manina, belle of the rocky coast. Eric attempts to double-cross Gérard by sailing without him; Manina saves Gérard from drowning when he attempts to pursue Eric, whose boat sinks together with the loot.

LE PORTRAIT DE SON PÈRE (The Image of his Father) 1953, France. Ninety-five minutes.

Production: Bertho-Films / Orsay Films *Director:* André Berthomieu *Script:* André Berthomieu and R Pierre *Photography:* Georges Million *Editor:* G Natot *Art director:* Raymond Negre *Music:* Henri Betti *Sound:* L Lacharmoise *Production manager:* G Cohen-Béat *Première:* 29th October 1953, Paris *British release details:* None *Leading players:* Jean Richard (Paul), Brigitte Bardot (Domino), and Michèle Philippe, Mona Goya,

Duvallès, M Nasil, P Faivre, Charles Bouillaud, Maurice Biraud, Philippe Mareuil, A Tanguy.

Story summary: Young farmer Paul is the bastard son of affluent businessman Durand. His father dies, leaving him his money and business. Paul goes to Paris and effects a remarkable transformation not only in the business but also in the attitudes of his stepsister Domino and even in his stepmother who reluctantly recognises Paul's qualities. Paul however realises this is not the life for him. He returns to his farm and marries his sweetheart.

ACT OF LOVE 1953, USA-France. One hundred and eight minutes.

Production: Benagoss Productions *Producer/Director:* Anatole Litvak *Script:* Irwin Shaw and Joseph Kessel, from the novel *The Girl in the Via Flaminia* by Alfred Hayes *Photography:* Armand Thirard *Editor:* Léonide Azar *Art director:* Alexandre Trauner *Music:* Michel Emer and Joe Hajos *Songs:* Michel Emer *Sound:* Jean de Bretagne *Production manager:* Pierre Laurent *Associate producer:* Georges Maurer *Assistant directors:* Michel Boisrond and Serge Vallin *Shooting:* 5th January–7th May 1953; exteriors at Villefranche-sur-Mer (Alpes-Maritimes) and Paris; interiors at Studios La Victorine (Nice), Studios Saint-Maurice and Joineville (Paris) *British release details:* distributed by United Artists, 1954, certificate 'A' *Leading players:* Kirk Douglas (Robert Teller), Dany Robin (Lisa), Barbara Laage (Nina), Serge Reggiani (Claude), Robert Strauss (Blackwood), Gabrielle Dorziat (Adèle), Gregoire Aslan (Commissaire), Marthe Mercadier (Young woman), Fernand Ledoux (Fernand), Brigitte Bardot (Mimi), George Mathews (Henderson), Leslie Dwyer (English sergeant).

Story summary: Robert Teller, an American soldier in Paris in 1944, meets Lisa, a hungry and homeless woman who agrees to share a room with him. Lisa falls in love with him, but it is only after she has been arrested on suspicion of black-market activities that Robert realises his own feelings for her. Robert seeks permission from his commanding officer to marry Lisa, but is refused and transferred to another area. He tries to find her but is arrested by the Military Police. Thinking he has deserted her, Lisa commits suicide. After the war, Robert returns to France on a sentimental journey.

SI VERSAILLES M'ÉTAIT CONTÉ 1953–54, France. Issued in English as *Versailles*. One hundred and sixty-five minutes.

Production: C L N Cocinex *Director:* Sacha Guitry *Script and dialogue:* Sacha Guitry *Photography:* Pierre Montazel (Eastman Colour) *Editor:* Raymond Lamy *Art director:* René Renoux *Costumes:* Monique Dumas *Music:* Jean Françaix *Sound:* Jo de Bretagne *Production manager:* Clément Duhour *Assistant director:* François Gir *Shooting:* begun on 6th July 1953; exteriors at Versailles *British release details:* distributed by Mondial Films, 1960, in a subtitled but slightly shortened version of one hundred and fifty-eight minutes, certificate 'A' *Leading players:* Sacha Guitry (Louis XIV), Georges Marchal (Young Louis XIV), Jean Marais (Louis XV), Claudette Colbert (Mme de Montespan), Micheline Presle (Mme de Pompadour), Giselle Pascal (Louise de la Vallière), Lana Marconi (Marie-Antoinette/Nicole Leguay), Fernand Gravey (Molière), Jean Desailly (Marivaux), Bernard Dhéran (Beaumarchais), Jean-Claude Pascal (Axel de Fersen), Orson Welles (Benjamin Franklin), Charles Vanel (de Vergennes), Gaby Morlay (Comtesse de la Motte), Gino Cervi (Cagliostro), Jean-Jacques Delbo (Comte de la Motte), Jean-Pierre Aumont (Cardinal de Rohan), Gérard Philipe (D'Artagnan), Jean-Louis Barrault (Fénelon), Maurice Teynac (M de Montespan), Edith Piaf (une tricoteuse), Yves Deniaud (peasant), Jean Tissier, Pierre

Larquey and Bourvil (museum guides), Gaston Rey (Henri IV),
Louis Arbessier (Louis XIII), Jean-Louis Alibert (Le Vau), Pierre
Lord (Mansart), Nicole Maurey (Mme de Fontanges), Mary
Marquet (Mme de Maintenon), Liliane Bert (Armande Béjart),
Georges Chamarat (La Fontaine), Samson Fainsilber (Mazarin),
Jeanne Boitel (Mme de Sévigné), Olivier Mathot (Boileau),
Jacques Varennes (Colbert), Gilbert Gil (Jean-Jacques Rousseau),
Lucien Nat (Montesquieu), Gilbert Boka (Louis XVI), Jacques
Berthier (Robespierre), Louis Seigner (Lavoisier), René Worms
(Bassange), Jacques Morel (Böhmer), Danièle Délorme (Louison
Chabray), Philippe Richard (Louis-Philippe), Michel Auclair
(Jacques Damiens), Brigitte Bardot (courtesan), Pauline Carton
(a neighbour), Jean Chevrier (Turenne), Aimé Clariond (Rivarol),
Nicole Courcel (Mme de Chalis), Daniel Gélin (Jean Collinet),
Jean Murat (Louvois), Jean Richard (Du Croisy), Tino Rossi
(gondolier), Germaine Rouer (Mlle Molière), Raymond Souplex
(commissionaire), and Renée Devillers, Claude Nollier, Paul
Colline, Anny Cordy, Duvaleix, Tania Fédor, Jacques François,
Jeanne Fusier-Gir, Constant Rémy, Howard Vernon, Emile
Drain, Gilles Quéant.

Story summary: A grandiose and sumptuous pageant of
Versailles and a cavalcade of French history, with authentic
settings and who's-who cast list of the French cinema.

TRADITÀ (Treachery) 1954, Italy. Issued in France as *Haine,
Amour et Trahison* (Hate, Love and Treachery). Ninety-eight
minutes.

Production: Flora Films *Director:* Mario Bonnard *Script:* from
a musical comedy by Jules Daccar *Photography:* Tonino Delli
Colli *Art director:* Piero Filippone *Music:* Jules Daccar *Production
manager:* Folco Laudati *British release details:* None *Leading
players:* Brigitte Bardot (Anna), Lucia Bosè (Elisabeth), Pierre

Cressoy (Franco), Giorgio Albertazzi (Enrico Alberti), and Camillo Pilotto, Henri Vidon, Tonio Selwart.

Story summary: During the First World War, Count Enrico Alberti who is of openly pro-Austrian sympathies, falls in love with Anna. His brother, Franco, is of opposite persuasion and a fervent patriot; a talented pianist he gives concerts throughout Italy and keeps in contact with the Italian insurrectionist movement. Franco is in love with singer Elisabeth, a Polish exile. But Anna falls in love with Franco, arousing the jealously of both Enrico and Elisabeth. They conspire to make Franco believe the police are after him, forcing him to flee. Italy enters into the war: Franco serves with the Italian army, Anna joins the Austrian Red Cross. Franco is captured. In hospital, he meets Anna who helps him to escape to the mountains. Enrico betrays him to the Austrians. Franco is condemned to death. To save his life, Elisabeth, who is still in love with him, helps Austrian agents capture a group of Italian saboteurs; the remorseful Enrico pretends to be the chief of the saboteurs, and is condemned to death in his brother's place. At war's end, Franco is released from prison to find happiness with Anna.

HELEN OF TROY 1954, USA. One hundred and eighteen minutes.

Production: Warner Bros *Director:* Robert Wise *Script:* John Twist, Hugh Gray and N Richard Nash *Photography:* Harry Stradling (Cinemascope and WarnerColor) *Editor:* Thomas Reilly *Art director:* Edward Carrere *Music:* Max Steiner *Sound:* Charles B Lang *Shooting:* spring, 1954 *British release details:* distributed by Warner Bros, 1956, one hundred and fourteen minutes, certificate 'U' *Leading players:* Rossana Podesta (Helen), Jacques Sernas (Paris), Sir Cedric Hardwicke (Priam), Stanley Baker (Achilles), Niall MacGinnis (Menelaus), Robert Douglas

(Agememnon), Torin Thatcher (Ulysses), Harry Andrews (Hector), Janette Scott (Cassandra), Ronald Lewis (Aeneas), Brigitte Bardot (Andraste).

Story summary: Spectacular production dealing with the wars between Troy and Greece, centering on the love of Helen, daughter of King Menelaus of Sparta, and Paris, son of King Priam of Troy. In an international but British-biased cast, Brigitte Bardot played a comparatively small role as a slave girl.

LE FILS DE CAROLINE CHÉRIE (The Son of Caroline Chérie) 1954, France. One hundred and ten minutes.

Production: Cinéphonic/SNEG (Gaumont) *Director:* Jean Devaivre, from the novel by Cécil Saint-Laurent *Photography:* Jean Lalier (Technicolor) *Editor:* Germaine Artus *Art director:* Jacques Krauss *Music:* Georges Van Parys *Sound:* Jean Rieul *Production manager:* Robert Sussfeld *Shooting:* 24th June–5th September 1954; exteriors at Roussillon; interiors at Studios Saint-Maurice *Première:* 11th March 1955, Paris *British release details:* None. *Leading players:* Jean-Claude Pascal (Juan d'Arandra), Jacques Dacqmine (Sallanches), Brigitte Bardot (Pilar), Magalie Noël (Teresa), Micheline Gary (Conchita), with Sophie Desmarets, Alfred Adam, Georges Descrières, Bernard Lajarrige, Daniel Ceccaldi, Maurice Escande, Marcel Perès, Michel Etcheverry, Dinan, Robert Manuel, Robert Le Béal, Robert Dalban, André Dumas, David Maxwell.

Story summary: The heroic and amorous adventures of Juan d'Arandra, son of Caroline Chérie, at the time of the French occupation of Spain under the First Empire.

FUTURES VEDETTES (Future Stars) 1954–55, France. Issued in English as *Sweet Sixteen.* Ninety-six minutes.

Production: Régie du Film/Del Duca *Director:* Marc Allégret

Script: Roger Vadim and Marc Allégret from a novel by Vicki Baum *Dialogue:* Roger Vadim and France Roche *Photography:* Robert Juillard *Editor:* Suzanne de Troeye *Art director:* Raymond Nègre *Music:* Jean Wiener *Sound:* Robert Biart *Production manager:* Claude Ganz *Assistant director:* P Boursaus *Shooting:* begun on 10th December 1954; interiors at Studios Saint-Maurice *British release details:* distributed by Gala Films, 1958, subtitled, certificate 'A' *Leading players:* Brigitte Bardot (Sophie), Jean Marais (Eric Walter), Denise Noël (Marie), Mischa Auer (Berger), Isabelle Pia (Elis), Yves Robert (Clément).

Story summary: Eric, an operatic tenor who has become a professor at the Vienna Conservatoire of Music, is the idol of the girl students. He is separated from his wife Marie, a career woman, but remains deeply in love with her. He seeks consolation in passing affairs, notably with two students, Sophie and Elis. Although friends, neither of the two girls is aware that the other is in love with Eric until Marie returns. Whereupon Eric forsakes them both and returns to his wife. The two girls find that their romantic suffering has increased their artistic abilities.

DOCTOR AT SEA 1955, Great Britain. Ninety-three minutes.

Production: Group Film Productions *Director:* Ralph Thomas *Producer:* Betty Box *Executive producer:* Earl St John *Script:* Nicholas Phipps, Jack Davies and Richard Gordon, from the novel by Richard Gordon *Photography:* Ernest Steward (Vista-Vision and Technicolor) *Editor:* Frederick Wilson *Art director:* Carmen Dillon *Music:* Bruce Montgomery *Song: Je ne sais pas* by Hubert Gregg *Sound recording:* John W Mitchell and Gordon K McCallum *British release details:* distributed by JARFID (J Arthur Rank Film Distributors), certificate 'U' *Leading players:* Dirk Bogarde (Simon), Brigitte Bardot (Helene Colbert), Brenda de Banzie (Muriel Mallet), James Robertson Justice

(Captain Hogg), Maurice Denham (Easter), Michael Medwin (Trail), Hubert Gregg (Archer), James Kenney (Fellowes), Raymond Huntley (Captain Beamish), Geoffrey Keen (Hornbeam), George Coulouris (Carpenter), Jill Adams (Jill), and Joan Sims, Noel Purcell, Cyril Chamberlain.

Story summary: Young doctor Simon wants to escape from his partner's daughter who is intent on marrying him. He signs on as ship's doctor on a cargo vessel – captained by a violent-tempered disciplinarian named Hogg. Simon finds numerous professional complications, plus some not-so-professional ones when the ship puts into a South American port. To the fury of the woman-hating Captain Hogg the vessel has two feminine passengers: cabaret singer Helene Colbert, and Muriel Mallet, the spinster daughter of the shipping line's chairman. Hogg's agitation increases when Muriel develops a positive affection for him. Simon winds up with Helen.

LES GRANDES MANOEUVRES 1955, France-Italy. Issued in English as *Summer Manoeuvres*. One hundred and six minutes.

Production: Filmsonor (Paris)-Rizzoli Film (Rome) *Director:* René Clair *Script:* René Clair, with the collaboration of Jérome Geronimi and Jean Marsan, from the novel by Courteline *Dialogue:* René Clair *Photography:* Robert Le Fèbvre and Robert Juillard (Eastman Colour) *Editor:* Louise Hautecoeur *Art director:* Léon Barsacq *Costumes:* Rosine Delamare *Music:* Georges Van Parys *Sound:* Antoine Petitjean *Production manager:* Jacques Planté *Second unit director:* Michel Boisrond *Assistant director:* Serge Vallin *Shooting:* 28th April–8th July 1955; interiors at Studios Boulogne *Première:* 1955, Venice Festival *British release details:* distributed by Films de France, 1956, certificate 'A' *Leading players:* Michèle Morgan (Marie-Louise Rivière), Gérard Philipe (Lt Armand de la Verne), Brigitte

Bardot (Lucie), Yves Robert (Félix), Jean Desailly (Victor Duverger), Pierre Dux (The Colonel), Jacques François (Rudolph), Lisa Delamare (Jeanne Duverger), Jacqueline Maillan (Juliette Duverger), Magali Noël (Thérèse, the singer), Simone Valère (Gisèle), Catherine Anouilh (Alice, the bride), Jacques Fabri (Armand's batman), Raymond Cordy (photographer), Olivier Hussenot (the prefect).

Story summary: Armand de la Verne, a cavalry officer stationed in a provincial town, has the reputation of being a Don Juan. He accepts a bet that within a month, before the regiment's departure for summer manoeuvres, he can become the lover of a woman chosen by chance. The woman selected is Marie-Louise Rivière, a divorcee who runs a hat-shop in the town. But Armand finds himself rebuffed; his flowers refused, his letters unopened. In time, however, Marie-Louise responds. Armand finds he has genuinely fallen in love with her and wants to forget the wager: instead of boasting of his victory, he declares his intention of marrying her. Unfortunately, Marie-Louise learns of the wager. In light of the circumstances and his reputation, she refuses to believe in his sincerity. Armand pleads with her to signify her forgiveness by opening her window next morning when the regiment passes by on its way to the summer manoeuvres. The window remains closed.

LA LUMIÈRE D'EN FACE 1955, France. Issued in English as *The Light Across the Street.* One hundred minutes.

Production: EGC (Enterprise Générale Cinématographique) *Director:* Georges Lacombe *Producer:* Jacques Gauthier *Script:* Louis Chavance and René Masson, from a story by Jean-Claude Aurel *Dialogue:* René Lefèvre *Photography:* Louis Page *Editor:* Raymond Leboursier *Art director:* Alexandre Trauner *Music:* Norbert Glanzberg *Sound:* Antoine Archimbaud *Production manager:* Fred Surin *Shooting:* begun on 11th July 1955; exteriors at Saint-Jean, Cap Ferrat, Cold'Eze and environs of Nice; interiors at Studios de la Victorine (Nice) *British release details:* distributed by Miracle Films, subtitled version, ninety-seven minutes, certificate 'X' *Leading players:* Raymond Pellegrin (Georges), Brigitte Bardot (Olivia), Roger Pigaut (Pietri), Claude Romain (Barbette), Guy Pierraud (Antoine), Lucien Hubert (Gaspard), Berval (Albert).

Story summary: Georges and Olivia, much in love, decide to marry. Olivia knows that there is no possibility of the marriage being consummated until Georges has recovered from a motor accident. They set up home in a transport cafe which they run between them. Georges becomes increasingly ill-tempered and difficult, obsessed by the belief that his wife has fallen for Pietri, the handsome, newly-arrived manager of the garage across the street. Georges tries to strangle her and Olivia flees to Pietri. Her husband fires at them both with a shotgun. In a mad frenzy he finally falls into the path of an incoming lorry and is killed.

CETTE SACRÉE GAMINE 1955, France. Originally to have been called *Mademoiselle Pigalle* and issued in English as *Mam'zelle Pigalle*. Eighty-six minutes.

Production: Lutétia / SLPF / Sonodis / SELB *Director:* Michel Boisrond *Script and dialogue:* Roger Vadim and Michel Boisrond, from an idea by Jean Périne *Photography:* Joseph Brun (Cinemascope and Eastman Colour) *Editor:* Jacques Mavel *Art director:* Jacques Chalvet *Music:* Henry Crolla and Hubert Rostaing *Sound:* Norbert Grenolle *Production manager:* Georges Sénamaud *Assistant director:* J Poitrenaud *Shooting:* begun on 6th September 1955; interiors at Franstudio (Saint-Maurice) *British release details:* distributed by Films de France, 1956, subtitled, certificate 'U' *Leading players:* Brigitte Bardot (Brigitte Latour), Jean

Bretonnière (Jean Cléry), Françoise Fabian (Lili), Bernard Lancret (Paul Latour), Raymond Bussières (Jérome), Mischa Auer (ballet master), Darry Cowl (man with the suitcase).

Story summary: Because he has a police record, night-club owner Paul Latour has to flee when he is wrongly suspected of forgery. He is worried that his daughter Brigitte, still at finishing school, will discover that he is not the shipping magnate he pretends he is. Jean Cléry, his friend and singing star at the club, comes to his assistance. He collects Brigitte from school, carefully keeping her away from the police. The situation gives rise to trouble with Jean's fiancée Lili. Brigitte finds she is in love with Jean. The pair become involved with the gang responsible for the forged notes. The truth comes out but all ends well: Paul is cleared, Brigitte is not bothered by the truth about her father, and Lili renounces Jean leaving the lovers free.

MIO FIGLIO NERONE (My Son Nero) 1956, Italy-France. Issued in France as *Les Week-Ends de Neron* and in English as *Nero's Weekend.* One hundred and five minutes.

Production: Titanus/Vides (Rome)–Les Films Marceau (Paris) *Director:* Steno *Script:* R Sonego, S Continenza, Diego Fabbri, Ugo Guerra, from a story by Steno *Photography:* Mario Bava (Cinemascope and Eastman Colour) *Art director:* Pietro Filippone *Music:* A F Lavagnino *British release details:* distributed by Gala Films, 1957, in a subtitled version, cut to ninety minutes, certificate 'A' *Leading players:* Brigitte Bardot (Poppea), Vittorio De Sica (Seneca), Gloria Swanson (Agrippina), Alberto Sordi (Nero), Giorgia Moll (Lidia), Ciccio Barbi (Anicetus).

Story summary: Roman Emperor Nero enjoys orgy-style feasts with his alluring young mistress Poppea. His enjoyment is interrupted by the unwelcome arrival of his mother Agrippina on what threatens to be a prolonged stay. Nero's ambition is to make music. Agrippina is determined to make him a military leader renowned in battle. Nero attempts to circumvent this by plotting to eliminate her by poison or by arranging for a stone to fall on her head. Agrippina in turn plots to kill Poppea with vipers in the bed, and to poison Nero's adviser Seneca. None of these homicidal attempts succeeds on either side. In the end, Nero decides he will be freer to make music without any of his unappreciative friends and relatives. He turns mother, mistress and adviser into stone busts. As a final gesture he sets fire to Rome which similarly had been guilty of not appreciating his music.

EN EFFEUILLANT LA MARGUERITE (Plucking the Daisy) 1956, France. Issued in English as *Mam'selle Striptease*. One hundred and one minutes.

Production: Films EGE/Hoche Productions *Director:* Marc Allégret *Producer:* Pierre Schwab *Script:* Roger Vadim and Marc Allégret, from an idea by William Benjamin *Dialogue:* Roger Vadim *Photography:* Louis Page *Editor:* Suzanne de Troeye *Art directors:* Alexandre Trauner and Auguste Capelier *Music:* Paul Misraki *Sound:* Jacques Carrère *Production manager:* Claude Ganz *Shooting:* begun on 13th February 1956; interiors at Studios Eclair *Première:* 5th October 1956, Paris *British release details:* distributed by Miracle Films, 1956, subtitled, certificate 'A' *Leading players:* Brigitte Bardot (Agnès), Daniel Gélin (Daniel), Robert Hirsch (Roger), Darry Cowl (Hubert), Nadine Tallier (Magali), Luciana Paoluzzi (Sophia), Mischa Auer (taxi driver), Jacques Dumesnil (Dumont), and Georges Chamarat, Anne Collette.

Story summary: General Dumont decides that some discipline is called for when he finds that his daughter, Agnès, has written a scandalous novel. Agnes eludes him and boards a train for Paris.

On the journey she meets a journalist named Daniel. In Paris, she goes to the house which she believes to be the home of her artist brother Hubert. She discovers that the house is the Balzac Museum, and that Hubert is the caretaker. Agnès runs into money trouble. She enters a striptease contest in the hope of winning the prize-money to settle her debts. She insists on remaining masked. Meantime, she and Daniel have become romantically involved. Daniel turns up at the contest. Agnès is furious when, unaware of the identity of the masked girl, Daniel tries to make love to her. The finals of the contest are held in her hometown, with her father among the adjudicators; Agnès persuades a friend to substitute for her. Finally, all her difficulties, financial and romantic, are smoothed out.

ET DIEU CRÉA LA FEMME (And God Created Woman) 1956, France. Issued in English as *And Woman . . . Was Created.* Ninety-one minutes.

Production: Iéna/UCIL/Cocinor *Director:* Roger Vadim *Producer:* Raoul Lévy *Script:* Roger Vadim and Raoul Lévy *Photography:* Armand Thirard (Cinemascope and Eastman Colour) *Editor:* Victoria Mercanton *Art director:* Jean André *Music:* Paul Misraki *Sound:* Pierre-Louis Calvet *Production manager:* Claude Ganz *Assistant director:* P Feyder *Shooting:* begun on 23rd April 1956; exteriors at Saint-Tropez *Première:* 28th November 1956, Paris *British release details:* distributed by Miracle Films, subtitled, ninety-one minutes, certificate 'X' *Leading players:* Brigitte Bardot (Juliette), Curd Jürgens (Eric), Jean-Louis Trintignant (Michel), Christian Marquand (Antoine), Georges Poujouly (Christian), Jeanne Marken (Mme Morin), Paul Faivre (M Morin), Marie Glory (Mme Tardieu), and Isabelle Cory, Claude Vega, Jean Lefebvre, Philippe Grenier, Jacqueline Ventura, Jean Tissier, Jane Mourey.

Story summary: Juliette, an orphan with natural sex-appeal and an inescapable attraction to men, lives in a small town with a childless couple, the Morins, and works in their bookshop. After associating with a wealthy shipyard owner, Eric, she becomes infatuated with the virile Antoine. She is dismayed to overhear him say he regards her merely as a passing amusement. She accepts a proposal of marriage by his gentle brother Michel. She finds herself falling in love with him and does her best to subdue her temperament and restlessness to make the marriage work. But, on meeting Antoine again, she succumbs to her old passion before running away. Michel fights with his brother and goes after his wife, finding that she has met Eric again. Eric, appreciating the situation, relinquishes her. Juliette returns home with Michel who remains madly in love with her.

LA MARIÉE EST TROP BELLE 1956, France. Issued in English as *The Bride is Too Beautiful*. Ninety-five minutes.

Production: Production Générale de Films/SN Pathé-Cinéma *Director:* Pierre Gaspard-Huit *Producer:* Christine Gouze-Renal *Script:* Philippe Agostini and Juliette Saint-Giniez, from the novel by Odette Joyeux *Dialogue:* Odette Joyeux *Photography:* Louis Page *Editor:* Louisette Hautecoeur *Art directors:* Jean d'Eaubonne and Pierre Duquesne *Music:* Norbert Glanzberg *Sound:* Antoine Archimbaud *Production manager:* Fred Surin *Assistant directors:* P Lary and S Vallin *Shooting:* begun on 15th July 1956 at Studios Paris, and on 6th August 1956 at Studios Boulogne *British release details:* distributed by Renown Pictures, 1957, subtitled, certificate 'A' *Leading players:* Brigitte Bardot (Chouchou), Micheline Presle (Judith), Louis Jourdan (Michel), Jean-François Calvé (Patrice), Marcel Amont (Toni), Roger Dumas (Marc), Madeleine Lambert (Aunt Agnes), Marcelle Arnold (Mme Victoire), Colette Regis (Aunt Yvonne).

Story summary: Judith and Michel, magazine proprietors, launch a young country girl, Catherine, into a career as a cover girl under the name of Chouchou. Patrice, a would-be actor who does some work for the magazine, falls for the girl, but she is smitten with Michel. When Michel persists in regarding her as a mere child, Chouchou determines to make him see that she is a grown woman. She flirts outrageously with Patrice. Her scheme eventually works. She and Michel marry in the village church.

UNE PARISIENNE 1957, France-Italy. Eighty-six minutes.

Production: Les Films Ariane/Cinetel/Filmsonor (Paris)–Rizzoli Film (Rome) *Director:* Michel Boisrond *Script:* Annette Wademant, Jean Aurel, Jacques Emmanuel and Michel Boisrond *Dialogue:* Annette Wademant *Photography:* Marcel Grignon (Technicolor) *Editor:* Claudine Bouché *Art director:* Jean André *Music:* Henri Crolla, Hubert Rostaing and André Hodeir *Sound:* Antoine Petitjean *Production manager:* Francis Cosne *Assistant director:* Jacques Poitrenaud *Shooting:* begun on 8th March 1957; interiors at Studios Billancourt *Première:* 16th December 1957, Paris *British release details:* distributed by Rank Film Distributors, 1959, subtitled, certificate 'A' *Leading players:* Brigitte Bardot (Brigitte), Henri Vidal (Michel), Charles Boyer (Prince Charles), André Luguet (Prime Minister Laurier), Nadia Gray (Queen Greta), Madeleine Lebeau (Monique), Claude Maurier (Caroline), Noël Roquevert (the husband).

Story summary: Appalled by finding his capricious daughter Brigitte in bed with his secretary Michel, the Prime Minister forces the pair to marry. Fortunately the two are in love, but Brigitte is peeved at her husband's reputation with women. She seizes an opportunity to get her own back by flirting with Prince Charles, who is on a state visit. The Prince enjoys the small, innocent flirtation with Brigitte in Nice before sending her back to her anxious husband, who remains puzzled by the entire episode.

LES BIJOUTIERS DU CLAIR DE LUNE (Moonlight Jewellers) 1957, France-Italy. Issued in English as *Heaven Fell That Night*. Ninety-five minutes.

Production: Iéna Productions/UCIL (Paris)–CEIAP (Rome) *Director:* Roger Vadim *Producer:* Raoul Lévy *Script:* Roger Vadim and Peter Viertel, from the novel by Albert Vidalie *Photography:* Armand Thirard (Cinemascope and Eastman Colour) *Editor:* Victoria Mercanton *Art director:* Jean André *Music:* Georges Auric *Sound:* Robert Biart *Production manager:* Roger Debelmas *Shooting:* begun on 28th June 1957; exteriors in Spain *Première:* 16th April 1958, Paris *British release details:* distributed by Columbia, 1958, subtitled, ninety minutes, certificate 'X' *Leading players:* Brigitte Bardot (Ursula), Alida Valli (Aunt Florentine), Stephen Boyd (Lambert), Pepe Nieto (Count Ribera), Maruchi Fresno (Conchita), Adriano Dominguez (Fernando), José Marco Davo (chief policeman), Antonio Vico (Count's driver).

Story summary: Ursula arrives in Spain to stay with uncle, Count Ribera, and Aunt Florentine. She is attracted to Lambert, a man bent on avenging his sister's suicide, for which he holds the Count responsible. After being beaten up by the Count's men, Lambert accidentally kills the Count. He spends the night with Florentine hoping to establish an alibi but she refuses to co-operate. Lambert flees with Ursula. The two are pursued by the police until Lambert, realising he has fallen in love with Ursula, decides to give himself up. In the confusion Ursula is accidentally killed.

EN CAS DE MALHEUR (In Case of Adversity) 1957, France-

Italy. Issued in English as *Love is My Profession*. One hundred and five minutes.

Production: Iéna/UCIL (Paris)–Incom (Rome) *Director:* Claude Autant-Lara *Producer:* Raoul J Lévy *Script:* Jean Aurenche and Pierre Bost, from the novel by Georges Simenon *Photography:* Jacques Natteau *Editor:* Madeleine Gug *Art director:* Max Douy *Music:* René Cloërec *Sound:* René Forget *Production managers:* Yves Laplanche and Roger Debelmas *Assistant directors:* Ghislaine Auboin and Michel Pazin *Shooting:* begun on 4th November 1957; exteriors in Paris; interiors at Studios Joinville *British release details:* distributed by Miracle Films, 1958, subtitled, certificate 'X' *Leading players:* Jean Gabin (André Gobillot), Brigitte Bardot (Yvette), Edwige Feuillère (Vivane Gobillot), Nicole Berger (Jeanine), Franco Interlenghi (Mazetti), Madeleine Barbulée (Bordenave), Jacques Clancy (Duret), Claude Magnier (Gaston).

Story summary: Gobillot, a middle-aged Parisian lawyer, secures the acquittal of a young street girl, Yvette, who had been involved in a hold-up. She, grateful, becomes his mistress. Gobillot finds in their relationship respite from the sedate respectability of his existence. In time, Yvette leaves him to return to a young student, Mazetti, with whom she is infatuated. Gobillot, whose preoccupation with the girl has affected both his matrimonial and professional life, goes in search of her. He finally finds her in an hotel room. She has been stabbed to death by her lover.

LA FEMME ET LE PANTIN (The Girl and the Puppet) 1958, France-Italy. Issued in English as *A Woman Like Satan*. One hundred and one minutes.

Production: Pro-Ge-Fi/Pathé-Cinéma/Gray Film (Paris); Dear Films (Rome) *Director:* Julien Duvivier *Script:* Jean Aurenche,

Julien Duvivier, Marcel Achard and Albert Valentin, from the novel by Pierre Loüys *Dialogue:* Marcel Achard *Photography:* Roger Hubert (Dyaliscope and Technicolor) *Editor:* Jacqueline Sadoul *Art director:* Georges Wakhévitch *Sound:* William Sivel *Production manager:* Fred Surin *Shooting:* begun on 8th April 1958; exteriors in Spain and the Camargue; interiors at Studios Boulogne *Première:* 13th February 1959, Paris *British release details:* distributed by United Artists, 1960, in a dubbed version reduced to eighty-five minutes, certificate 'X' *Leading players:* Brigitte Bardot (Eva), Antonio Vilar (Don Matteo Diaz), Espanita Cortez (Maria-Teresa), Jacques Mauclair (Stanislas Marchand), Dario Moreno (Arabadjian), Michel Roux (Albert), Lila Kedrova (Manuela), Jess Hahn (Sidney), Claude Goddard (Mercédès), and Germaine Michel, Rivers Cadet.

Story summary: Don Matteo, a rich middle-aged landowner, becomes infatuated with a young girl, Eva. He goes every night to the dingy club where she dances. Eva plays hard to get. Don Matteo surprises her dancing nude before strangers, but her ingenuousness dispels his anger. He leaves wife and home to follow her when she goes on tour in the provinces with a second-rate flamenco company. He becomes jealous of her handsome dancing partner. Having been kept dangling for so long the humiliated man goes berserk. Eva at last decides to become his mistress.

BABETTE S'EN VA-T-EN GUERRE 1959, France. Issued in English as *Babette Goes to War*. One hundred and three minutes.

Production: Iéna/Films Ariane *Director:* Christian-Jaque *Producer:* Raoul Lévy *Script:* Raoul Lévy, Gérard Oury, Jean Ferry and Jacques Emmanuel *Dialogue:* Michel Audiard *Photography:* Armand Thirard (Cinemascope and Eastman Colour) *Editor:* Jacques Desagneaux *Art director:* Jean André *Music:* Gilbert

Bécaud *Sound:* William Robert Sivel *Production manager:* Louis Wipf *Shooting:* begun on 14th January 1959; exteriors in London; interiors at Studios Joinville *Première:* 18th September 1959, Paris *British release details:* distributed by Columbia (released 11th January 1960), in a dubbed version, ninety-eight minutes, certificate 'A' *Leading players:* Brigitte Bardot (Babette), Jacques Charrier (Gérard), Hannes Messemer (Von Arenberg), Yves Vincent (Capitaine Darcy), Ronald Howard (Fitzpatrick), Francis Blanche (Schulz), René Havard (Louis), Jacques Hilling (Capitaine), Alain Bouvette (Emile), Charles Bouillaud (Pierrot), Max Elloy (Firmin), Pierre Bertin (Le Duc), Viviane Gosset (La Duchesse), Mona Goya (Mme Fernande), Noël Roquevert (Gustave).

Story summary: Country girl Babette, a refugee in Britain in 1940, volunteers to serve with the Free French as a housemaid. But she is sent by British Intelligence to Paris, as part of a plot to kidnap a German General. She is suspected by the Gestapo. They force her to spy on the General who is himself suspected of being a traitor. Babette plays a double game in which she satisfies British Intelligence and has romantic compensation for her trouble.

VOULEZ-VOUS DANSER AVEC MOI? (Won't You Dance With Me?) 1959, France-Italy. Issued in English as *Come Dance With Me.* Ninety-one minutes.

Production: Francos Films (Paris); Vides (Rome) *Director:* Michel Boisrond *Producer:* Francis Cosne *Script:* Annette Ademant, L C Thomas, Jean-Charles Tacchella, Michel Boisrond and Francis Cosne, from the novel *The Blonde Died Dancing* by Kelley Roos *Dialogue:* Annette Wademant *Photography:* Robert Lefebvre (Technicolor) *Editor:* Claudine Bouché *Art director:* Jean André *Music:* Henri Crolla and André Hodeir *Sound:*

William Sivel *Assistant director:* J Poitrenaud *Shooting:* begun on 15th July 1959; interiors at Studios La Victorine (Nice) *Première:* 18th December 1959, Paris *British release details:* distributed by Columbia, 1960 (release date, 26th September 1960), subtitled, certificate 'X' *Leading players:* Brigitte Bardot (Virginie), Henri Vidal (Hervé), Dawn Addams (Anita), Noël Roquevert (Albert), Dario Moreno (Flores), Philippe Nicaud (Daniel), Paul Frankeur (Inspector), Serge Gainsbourg (Léon), and Pascal Mazotti, François Chaumette, Maria Pacaume.

Story summary: Virginie, daughter of wealthy irascible industrialist Albert Decauville-Lachenée, marries young dentist Hervé Dandieu against her father's wishes. Following a domestic quarrel, Hervé goes to a bar where he meets Anita. She is a blackmail specialist and adds Hervé to her victims. Arriving at a dance hall to keep an appointment with Anita, Hervé finds her dead: beside her is his own gun. Virginie, unaware that Hervé was being blackmailed, believes in her husband's innocence. Determined to find the real murderer, she gets a job at the dance-hall as a dancing instructress. There is no lack of suspects, all of them Anita's blackmail victims. She finally succeeds in identifying the murderer: a homosexual performer in a club for perverts.

LE TESTAMENT D'ORPHÉE 1959, France. Eighty-three minutes.

Production: Editions Cinégraphiques/Films du Carrosse *Director and script:* Jean Cocteau *Producer:* Jean Thuillier *Photography:* Roland Pontoizeau *Editor:* Marie Josephe Yoyotte *Costumes and sculptures:* Janine Janet *Music:* Georges Auric and Martial Solal; also music by Gluck, Handel and Wagner *Sound:* Pierre Bertrand *Production manager:* Irénée Leriche *Première:* 18th February 1960, Paris *British release details:* distributed by Gala Films, 1960, in a version with English narration by Michael Goodliffe, certificate

'A' *Leading players:* Jean Cocteau (the poet), Maria Casarès (the princess), François Périer (Heurtebise), Edouard Dermit (Cégeste), Henri Crémieux (the scientist), Jean-Pierre Léaud (the child), Jean Marais (Oedipus), Yul Brynner (the doorman), Nicole Courcel (nursemaid), Daniel Gélin (the assistant), Claudine Oger (Minerva) Georges Chretelain and Michèle Lemoigne (the lovers), and Jacqueline Roque, Charles Aznavour, Françoise Christophe, Lucia Bosé, Henry Torrès, Pablo Picasso, Luis-Miguel Dominguin Serge Lifar, Françoise Arnoul, Françoise Sagan, Brigitte Bardot, Roger Vadim, Annette Stroyberg, Mme Weisweiler.

Story summary: A personal, surrealist fantasy by Jean Cocteau, with Brigitte Bardot and Roger Vadim among those making brief appearances.

LA VÉRITÉ (The Truth) 1960, France-Italy. Issued in English as *La Vérité*. One hundred and thirty minutes.

Production: Iéna (Paris); CEIAP (Rome) *Director:* Henri-Georges Clouzot *Producer:* Raoul J Lévy *Script and dialogue:* Henri-Georges Clouzot, Jérome Géronimi, Simone Drieu, Michèle Perrein and Christiane Rochefort *Photography:* Armand Thirard *Editor:* Albert Jurgenson *Art director:* Jean André *Music:* excerpts from Stravinsky (*The Firebird*) and Beethoven *Sound:* William R Sivel *Production manager:* Louis Wipf *Shooting:* begun on 2nd May 1960; interiors at Studios Joinville *Première:* 2nd November 1960, Paris *British release details:* distributed by BLC (Columbia), 1962, in both subtitled and dubbed versions, one hundred and twenty five minutes, certificate 'X' *Leading players:* Brigitte Bardot (Dominique Marceau), Marie-José Nat (Annie Marceau), Sami Frey (Gilbert Tellier), Charles Vanel (Maître Guérin), Paul Meurisse (prosecuting counsel), Jacqueline Porel (woman lawyer), Louis Seigner (president of the court), René Blancard (attorney), Jean-Louis Reynolds (Michel), André

Oumansky (Ludovic), Fernand Ledoux (court physician), Arbessier (conservatory professor), and Jacques Perrin, Claude Berri, Barbara Sohmers, Suzy Wills, Christian Lude.

Story summary: Dominique is on trial for murdering her lover, Gilbert. The circumstances leading up to the crime are shown in flashback. Dominique and her sister Annie are of opposite temperaments: Annie is virtuous, a student of the violin at the Paris Conservatoire; Dominique is shiftless, a problem to her parents, and involved with a good-for-nothing Latin Quarter crowd. Dominique has a tempestuous affair with Annie's friend Gilbert Tellier, who is studying at the Conservatoire to become a conductor; after a jealous quarrel they break off their relationship. Later, embarked on his career, Gilbert takes up with Annie again. They become engaged. Dominique now has regrets about breaking with Gilbert and becomes his mistress. Finally Gilbert realises she means nothing to him and rejects her completely. Enraged, Dominique shoots him and makes an unsuccessful suicide attempt. Her protestations of love for Gilbert make no impression on the judges. Dominique commits suicide in her cell.

AGNÈS BERNAUER episode in AMOURS CÉLÈBRES (Famous Love Affairs) 1961, France-Italy.

Production: Générale Européenne de Films/Unidex Production (Paris); Cosmos Films (Rome) *Director:* Michel Boisrond *Producer:* Gilbert Bokanowski *Script:* France Roche *Adaptation and dialogue:* Jacques Prévert *Photography:* Robert Lefebvre *Editor:* Raymond Lamy *Art directors:* Georges Wakhévitch and Lila de Nobili *Music:* Maurice Jarre *Sound:* William Sivel *Production manager:* Armand Bécué *Première:* 3rd November 1961, Paris *British release details:* None *Leading players:* Brigitte Bardot (Agnès), Alain Delon (Albert), Pierre Brasseur (Wittelsbach), and Jean-Claude Brialy, Suzanne Flon, Michel Etcheverry,

Jacques Dumesnil.

Story summary: Agnès Bernauer is the last of the four episodes which constitute the film. Agnes, a girl of humble birth, is secretly married to the Prince of Bavaria but becomes the victim of court intrigues and jealousies. Condemned to death for alleged witchcraft, she is thrown into the river; her husband elects to die too.

VIE PRIVÉE (Private Life) 1961, France-Italy. Issued in English as *A Very Private Affair*. One hundred and three minutes.

Production: Progefi/Cipra (Paris); CCM (Rome) *Director:* Louis Malle *Producer:* Christine Gouze-Renal *Script:* Louis Malle, Jean-Paul Rappeneau, J Ferry *Dialogue:* Jean-Paul Rappeneau *Photography:* Henri Decaë (Eastman Colour) *Editor:* Kenout Peltier *Art director:* Bernard Evein *Music:* Fiorenzo Carpi *Sound:* William R Sivel *Production manager:* Fred Surin *British release details:* distributed by MGM, 1962, in a dubbed version reduced to ninety-four minutes, certificate 'A' *Leading players:* Brigitte Bardot (Jill), Marcello Mastroianni (Fabio), Grégoire von Rezzori (Gricha), Eléanora Hirt (Cécile), Ursula Kubler (Carla), Dirk Sanders (Dick), Paul Sorèze (Maxime), Antoine Roblot (Alain), Jacqueline Doyen (Juliette), Nicolas Bataille (Edmond), Jean Allard (charwoman), Mario Naldi (Italian grocer), François Marié (François), Christian de Tillière (Albert), Gilles Quéant (Tovar), Elie Presman (Olivier), Louis Malle (a journalist).

Story summary: Jill leaves Geneva to follow her boy friend to Paris, largely to escape from her attraction for stage director Fabio, husband of her best friend Carla. She begins a successful career, first as a model, then as a cover girl, and finally as a film star. But her fame, together with notoriety after a succession of lovers, becomes a burden, allowing her no privacy. Driven to a nervous breakdown, she returns to Switzerland where she finds that Fabio and Carla have separated. Jill and Fabio fall in love, and she at last finds personal happiness. A peaceful period of seclusion ends when Fabio returns to Spoleto to produce a play. Jill follows him there, but renewed contact with the outside world and exposure again to the glare of publicity make their romance increasingly difficult, leading to Jill's tragic death.

LE REPOS DU GUERRIER (Warrior's Rest) 1962, France-Italy. Issued in English as *Warrior's Rest*. One hundred and two minutes.

Production: Francos Film (Paris); Incei Film (Rome) *Director:* Roger Vadim *Producer:* Francis Cosne *Script:* Claude Choublier and Roger Vadim, from the novel by Christiane Rochefort *Dialogue:* Roger Vadim *Photography:* Armand Thirard (Franscope and Eastman Colour) *Editor:* Victoria Mercanton *Art director:* Jean André *Music:* Michel Magne *Sound:* Robert Biart *Production manager:* Paul Joly *Shooting:* begun on 5th February 1962; interiors at Studios Billancourt *Première:* 5th September 1962, Paris *British release details:* distributed by Gala Films, subtitled, ninety-nine minutes, certificate 'X' *Leading players:* Brigitte Bardot (Geneviève Le Theil), Robert Hossein (Renaud Sarti), James Robertson Justice (Katov), Macha Méril (Raphaele), Jacqueline Porel (Geneviève's mother), Jean-Marc Bory (Pierre), Jean-Marc Tennberg (Coco), Michel Serrault (Lawyer Varange), Ursula Kubler (nurse), Robert Dalban (Police Sergeant in Paris), Jean Tuscano (jazz musician).

Story summary: Geneviève, a rich girl in her mid-twenties, finds the calm and reassuring world in which she has hitherto lived shattered when she falls deeply in love with Sarti, an alcoholic waster who has attempted suicide. He maltreats her, but Geneviève stoically suffers degradation for the sake of love.

On a trip to Italy, Sarti blatantly takes up with a tart. Geneviève leaves him. After much soul-searching, Sarti returns to her. Geneviève takes him back.

LE MÉPRIS (Contempt) 1963, France-Italy. One hundred and three minutes.

Production: Films Concordia/Rome Paris Film (Paris); Compania Cinematografica Champion (Rome) *Director:* Jean-Luc Godard *Producers:* Georges de Beauregard, Carlo Ponti and Joseph E Levine *Script and dialogue:* Jean-Luc Godard, from the novel *Il Disprezzo* by Alberto Moravia *Photography:* Raoul Coutard (Franscope and Technicolor) *Editors:* Agnès Guillemot and Lila Lakshmanan *Art director:* (none) *Costumes:* Tanine Autre *Music:* Georges Delerue *Sound:* William Sivel *Production managers:* Philippe Dussart and Carlo Lastricati *Assistant director:* Charles Bitsch *Shooting:* begun on 22nd April 1963; exteriors in Italy *Première:* 20th December 1963, Paris *British release details:* distributed by Avco Embassy, 1970, subtitled, certificate 'X' *Leading players:* Brigitte Bardot (Camille Javal), Jack Palance (Jeremy Prokosh), Michel Piccoli (Paul Javal), Giorgia Moll (Francesca Vanini), Fritz Lang (himself), Jean-Luc Godard (assistant director), Linda Véras (Siren).

Story summary: Camille is happily married to successful playwright Paul, who is currently working on a project with American producer Jeremy Prokosh. Suddenly and unaccountably, Camille finds that her love for her husband has waned: passion has been replaced by indifference. Paul desperately tries to understand Camille's change of heart. Jeremy, who is organising a film production of the Odyssey to be scripted by Paul and directed by Fritz Lang, takes the company to Capri. Jeremy begins to pay court to Camille. Disagreements and difficulties arise concerning the script which itself parallels the real-life situation. Camille, now openly contemptuous of Paul, rejects his plea to return with him to the life they once knew. She decides instead to return to Rome by car with Prokosh. The car crashes; Camille and Prokosh are killed. Paul returns to his work in the theatre; Fritz Lang proceeds with the film.

UNE RAVISSANTE IDIOTE (A Ravishing Idiot) 1963, France-Italy. Issued in English as *A Ravishing Idiot;* occasionally known as *Adorable Idiot* or *Bewitching Scatterbrain.* One hundred and eight minutes.

Production: Belles Rives (Paris); Flora Film (Rome) *Director:* Edouard Molinaro *Producer:* Michel Ardan *Script:* Edouard Molinaro and Georges André Tabet, from the novel by Charles Exbrayat *Dialogue:* Georges André Tabet *Photography:* Andréas Winding *Editor:* Robert Isnardon *Art directors:* Jean André and Robert Clavel *Music:* Michel Legrand *Sound:* Robert Biart *Assistant director:* Pierre Cosson *Shooting:* begun on 21st October 1963; interiors at Studios Billancourt *Première:* 13th March 1964, Paris *British release details:* distributed by Gala Films, 1966, in a dubbed version, ninety-nine minutes, certificate 'U' *Leading players:* Brigitte Bardot (Penelope Lightfeather), Anthony Perkins (Harry Compton), Grégoire Aslan (Bagda), Denise Provence (Lady Barbara Dumphreys), André Luguet (Sir Reginald Dumphreys), Hans Verner (Farrington), Charles Millot (Balaniev), Jean-Marc Tennberg (Cartwright), Hélène Dieudonné (Mamy), Jacques Monod (surgeon), Paul Demange (bank manager).

Story summary: Harry Compton, a young spy, is attracted to Marxist Leninism while enjoying the fruits of capitalism. His current assignment is in London. He is out to obtain a secret Admiralty file for Bagda, an important link in the Soviet spy network. His particular problem is to get to know Sir Reginald

Dumphreys, head of Admiralty security, who has custody of the file. Having fallen for Penelope Lightfeather, [who is dressmaker to Lady Barbara Dumphreys: a confirmed gossip] they contrive to be at a reception in Sir Reginald's home. There the file disappears more than once before the situation sorts itself out to the gratification of nearly everybody concerned.

PAPARAZZI 1963, France. Twenty-two minutes.

Production: Films du Colisée *Director/script/editor:* Jacques Rozier *Commentary spoken by:* Michel Piccoli, Jean Lescot and David Tonelli *Photography:* Maurice Perrimond *Music:* Antoine Duhamel.

Story summary: A short film about the Paparazzi – Italian news photographers who plague celebrities – in which Brigitte Bardot, Jean-Luc Godard and Michel Piccoli made appearances. Not distributed in Britain.

VIVA MARIA! 1965, France–Italy. One hundred and twenty minutes.

Production: Nouvelles Editions de Films/Productions Artistes Associés (Paris); Vides (Rome) *Director:* Louis Malle *Producers:* Oscar Dancigers and Louis Malle *Script:* Louis Malle and Jean-Claude Carrière *Photography:* Henri Decaë (Panavision and Eastman Colour) *Editors:* Kenout Peltier and Suzanne Baron *Art director:* Bernard Evein *Special effects:* Lee Zavitz *Music and musical direction:* Georges Delerue *Lyrics:* Louis Malle and Jean-Claude Carrière *Costumes:* Ghislain Ihry *Sound:* José B Carles *Production managers:* Alain Queffelean and Pascal Aragones *Assistant directors:* Volker Schloendorff, Manuel Muñoz and Juan-Luis Buñuel *Shooting:* begun on 26th January 1965; exteriors in Mexico *British release details:* distributed by United Artists, 1966, subtitled, certificate 'A' *Leading players:* Jeanne

Moreau (Maria I), Brigitte Bardot (Maria II), George Hamilton (Florès), Gregor Von Rezzori (Diogène), Paulette Dubost (Mme Diogène), Claudio Brook (Rodolfo), Carlos Lopez Moctezuma (Rodrigues), Poldo Bendandi (Werther), Francisco Reiguera (Father Superior), Jonathan Eden (Juanito), Adriana Roel (Janine), José-Angel Espinoza (El Presidente), José Baviera (Don Alvaro), Fernando Wagner (Maria II's father), José Luis Campa, Roberto Campa, Eduardo Murillo and José Esqueda (The 'Turcos').

Story summary: Maria Fitzgerald O'Malley is stranded in Central America when her Irish anarchist father is killed in one of their explosives exploits against the British. She finds her way into a troupe of travelling players, among whom is Maria, a singer whose partner in a double act has just committed suicide. The singer (Maria I) engages the Irish girl (Maria II) as her new partner. By accident their act turns into a striptease affair; it is such a success they keep it that way. During their travels, they witness the brutality with which wealthy landowners treat the oppressed peasants. Maria I falls in love with Florès, a revolutionary leader. When Florès dies, she promises to continue the revolution he has started. Her abilities are not at first the equal of her intentions; but with the help of the troupe, and in particular of Maria II, she makes her mark on the land. However, both Marias fall into the hands of the Inquisition, whose rusty and long-neglected instruments of torture fail to work. The two evade their captors and successfully accomplish the revolution before heading towards Europe.

DEAR BRIGITTE 1965, USA. One hundred minutes.
Production: Fred Kohlmar Productions *Producer/director:* Henry Koster *Script:* Hal Kanter, from the novel *Erasmus with Freckles* by John Haase *Photography:* Lucien Ballard (Cinemascope and DeLuxe Colour) *Editor:* Marjorie Fowler *Art directors:* Jack

177

Martin Smith and Malcolm Brown *Music:* George Duning *Sound:* Alfred Bruzlin and Elmer Raguse *Special photographic effects:* L B Abbott and Emil Kosa Jr *Assistant director:* Fred R Simpson *British release details:* distributed by 20th Century-Fox, 1965, certificate 'U' *Leading players:* James Stewart (Robert Leaf), Fabian (Kenneth), Glynis Johns (Vina), Cindy Carol (Pandora), Billy Mumy (Erasmus), John Williams (Upjohn), Jack Kruschen (Dr Volker), Charles Robinson (George), Howard Freeman (Dean Sawyer), Jane Wald (Terry), Alice Pearce (unemployment clerk), Jesse White (Argyle), Gene O'Donnell (Lt Rink), Ed Wynn (The Captain), Orville Sherman (Von Scholgg), Maida Severn (schoolteacher), Pitt Herbert (bank manager), Adair Jameson (saleslady), Marcelle de la Brosse (taxi driver), and Brigitte Bardot (herself).

Story summary: Erasmus, the eight-year-old son of boat-dwelling Professor Leaf, is a mathematical prodigy who unfailingly predicts horse-race winners and is mad about Brigitte Bardot. Because his father has been duped by a confidence trickster, the boy's talent is exploited by a crooked organisation. Professor Leaf takes his son to Paris where the boy meets his adored Brigitte in person. On their return home, Leaf discovers the truth about the trickery, and puts an end to it. But he stakes the family bankroll on one final fling. Thanks to Erasmus's accurate prediction, they win a large sum.

A COEUR JOIE (Two Weeks in September) 1966, France-Great Britain. Ninety-five minutes.

Production: Francos Films/Les Films du Quadrangle/Les Films Pomereu (Paris); Kenwood Films (London) *Director:* Serge Bourguignon *Producers:* Francis Cosne and Kenneth Harper *Script:* Vahé Katcha, Pascal Jardin and Serge Bourguignon (English adaptation by Sean Graham) *Photography:* Edmond

Séchan (Franscope and Eastman Colour) *Editor:* Jean Ravel *Art director:* Rino Mondellini *Costumes:* Tanine Autre *Music:* Michel Magne *Sound:* William Sivel *Shooting:* begun on 5th September 1966; exteriors in London and Scotland; interiors at Studios Billancourt *British release details:* distributed by Rank Film Distributors, 1967, in an English version, certificate 'X' *Leading players:* Brigitte Bardot (Cécile), Laurent Terzieff (Vincent), Jean Rochefort (Philippe), James Robertson Justice (McClintock), Michael Sarne (Dickinson), Georgina Ward (Patricia), Carol Lebel (Monique), Annie Nicolas (Chantal), Murray Head (Dickinson's assistant).

Story summary: Photographic model Cécile feels that her relationship with her lover, a publisher named Philippe, is not all it should be. She accepts an assignment in London where she is persistently wooed by Vincent, a young geologist. The two holiday in Scotland. Returning to London, Cécile has to choose between her two lovers, for Philippe is on his way from Paris. Vincent hopes to settle the matter by urging her to join him aboard a plane bound for Hong Kong; Cécile vacillates. By the time she has decided to choose Vincent, the plane has taken off.

WILLIAM WILSON episode in HISTOIRES EXTRA-ORDINAIRES (Extraordinary Tales) 1967, France-Italy. The complete film is also known as *Spirits of the Dead*.

Production: Les Films Marceau/Cocinor (Paris); PEA (Rome) *Director:* Louis Malle *Script:* Louis Malle and Daniel Boulanger *Photography:* Tonino delli Colli *Music:* Nino Rota *Shooting:* begun on 20th March 1967; exteriors in Rome *Première:* 14th June 1968, Paris *British release details:* None *Leading players:* Alain Delon (William Wilson), Brigitte Bardot (Giuseppina), and Katia Cristina, Umberto d'Orsi.

Story summary: An adaptation of the story by Edgar Allan Poe,

William Wilson is one of three episodes which constitute the film. Set in 19th century Italy, the tale concerns a proud and cruel officer who has a card-game encounter with a strange young woman and is haunted by his Doppelgänger.

SHALAKO 1968, Great Britain. One hundred and thirteen minutes.

Production: Kingston Films: A Dimitri de Grunwald Production *Director:* Edward Dmytryk *Producer:* Euan Lloyd *Script:* J J Griffith, Hal Hopper and Scot Finch, from the novel by Louis L'Amour; film story by Clark Reynolds *Photography:* Ted Moore (Franscope and Technicolor) *2nd unit photography:* John Cabrera *Editor:* Bill Blunden *Art director:* Herbert Smith *Special effects:* Michael Collins *Music:* Robert Farnon *Musical direction:* Muir Mathieson *Title song lyrics:* Jim Dale *Sound:* Keith Palmer *Associate producer:* Hal Mason *Production manager:* Ronnie Bear *Assistant directors:* Peter Price and Joe Ochoa *British release details:* distributed by Warner-Pathé, 1969, certificate 'A' *Leading players:* Sean Connery (Shalako), Brigitte Bardot (Irina Lazaar), Stephen Boyd (Bosky Fulton), Jack Hawkins (Sir Charles Daggett), Peter Van Eyck (Frederick von Hallstatt), Honor Blackman (Lady Daggett), Woody Strode (Chato), Eric Sykes (Mako), Alexander Knox (Henry Clarke), Valerie French (Elena Clarke), Julian Mateos (Rojas), Donald Barry (Buffalo), Rodd Redwing (Chato's father), 'Chief' Elmer Smith (Loco), Hans De Vries (Hans), Walter Brown (Peter Wells), Charles Stalnaker (Marker), Bob Cunningham (Luther), John Clark (Hockett), Bob Hall (Johnson).

Story summary: Countess Irina Lazaar is among a party of European aristocrats on a hunting safari in New Mexico in 1880. Their guide, Bosky Fulton, has deliberately led them into Apache territory. Irina is saved from falling victim to Indians by the intervention of Shalako who promises the Apache chief that he will have the hunters out of Indian territory by sun-up. The Europeans obstinately refuse to be browbeaten by Apache threats. The situation results in the massacre of some of the party, the scaling of mountain slopes by the rest to make a defensive stand on the plateau, and the final resolution of the battle by Shalako in Indian-style combat with the Apache chief's son. Shalako wins but spares his opponent's life. While the remnants of the expedition return homewards, Irina rides off with Shalako.

LES FEMMES (The Women) 1969, France-Italy. Ninety minutes.

Production: Lira Films (Paris); Ascot Cineraid (Rome) *Director:* Jean Aurel *Script:* Cécil Saint-Laurent and Jean Aurel *Dialogue:* Cécil Saint-Laurent *Photography:* Jean-Marc Ripert (Eastman Colour) *Editor:* Anne-Marie Coteret *Art director:* Armand Labussière *Music:* Luis Fuentès Jr *Sound:* Jean Petit *Production manager:* Ralph Baum *Assistant director:* Meyer Berreby *Shooting:* begun on 24th March 1969; exteriors at Paris and Versailles *British release details:* None *Leading players:* Brigitte Bardot (Clara), Maurice Ronet (Jérôme), Tanya Lopert (Louise), Patrick Gilles (Raphaël), Jean-Pierre Marielle (The Editor), Christina Holm (Marianne), Annie Duperey (Hélène), Carole Lebel (Gertrude).

Story summary: In her business life, Clara is a secretary seeking a new job; in her private life she is becoming dissatisfied with her lover, Raphaël. In his professional life, Jérôme is a writer, famous since winning a prize; in his private life he is much a ladies' man with a double attachment − to Hélène and Marianne. Jérôme is planning to leave Paris for peace and quiet in order to write a book, and needs a secretary. His requirements, however, extend to something above and beyond normal secretarial duties. Clara presents herself for the job. Discovering the conditions of contract, she is indignant . . . but accepts the appointment nevertheless. Raphaël sees her off at the station; aboard the train, Clara and Jérôme begin their relationship as agreed. Clara falls for Jérôme, becoming possessive and aggressive, successfully eliminating her two rivals. She finally becomes dissatisfied with her lover. When she packs up and leaves him, Jérôme feels empty and sad – but snaps out of it by taking another attractive secretary.

L'OURS ET LA POUPÉE (The Bear and the Doll) 1969, France.

Production: Parc Film/Marianne Productions *Director:* Michel Deville *Producer:* Mag Bodard *Script:* Nina Companeez and Michel Deville *Adaptation and dialogue:* Nina Companeez *Photography:* Claude Lecomte (Eastman Colour) *Editor:* Nina Companeez *Music:* Rossini, Eddie Vartan *Sound:* André Hervé *Production manager:* Philippe Dussart *Assistant director:* Jean Lefèvre *Shooting:* begun on 29th May 1969; exteriors in Paris; completed on 6th August 1969 *Première:* 4th February 1970, Paris *British release details:* None *Leading players:* Brigitte Bardot (Félicia), Jean-Pierre Cassel (Gaspard), Daniel Ceccaldi (Ivan), Xavier Gélin (Reginald), Georges Claisse (Stéphane), Patrick Gilles (Titus).

Story summary: 'The Bear' is Gaspard, a thirty-five-year-old cellist in a radio orchestra; he is absentminded and uncouth, and cares only about music, flowers, living in the country, and his family. 'The Doll' is Félicia, rich and fashionable, divorced, flirtatious, spoiled, insufferable but irresistible. On the rainy morning that Félicia sets off in her Rolls to obtain her second divorce, she is involved in an accident at a crossroads near Bourgival. Her victim is Gaspard. The two dislike each other so much that they find it necessary to meet again to make their animosity explicit. Félicia, unused to encountering resistance to her charm, sees a challenge in his opposition and decides to captivate Gaspard. There ensues a head-on clash between two completely different personalities and life-styles, with obstinacy as a common trait.

LES NOVICES (The Novices) 1970, France-Italy. Ninety-five minutes.

Production: Les Films La Boétie (Paris); Rizzoli (Rome) *Director:* Guy Casaril *Producer:* André Génovès *Script and adaptation:* Guy Casaril *Dialogue:* Paul Gégauff *Photography:* Claude Lecomte (Eastman Colour) *Editor:* Nicole Gauduchon *Art director:* (none) *Music:* François de Roubaix *Sound:* Guy Chichignoud *Production manager:* Georges Casati *Assistant director:* Marc Picaud *Shooting:* begun on 1st June 1970; exteriors in Paris *Première:* 28th October 1970, Paris *British release details:* distributed by Scotia-Barber, 1971, dubbed version, ninety minutes, certificate 'X' *Leading players:* Brigitte Bardot (Agnès), Annie Girardot (Mona Lisa), Lucien Barjon (ambulance client), Angelo Bardi (village client), Jean Carmet (client with dog), Monsieur Deus (priest), Jacques Duby (ambulance driver), Jess Hahn (American client), Jacques Jouanneau (client), Clément Michu (stuttering client), Antonio Passalia (playboy), Jean Roquel (taxi driver), Noël Roquevert (old client).

Story summary: While her sister nuns from a Brittany convent are enjoying a swim in the sea, Sister Agnès steals clothes and a bicycle and makes her way to Paris. She is befriended by prostitute, Mona Lisa, who invites Agnès to share her apartment. To earn a living, Agnès decides to become a prostitute too. Despite Mona Lisa's tuition she is unsuccessful and becomes an ambulance driver instead. The two conceive the idea of turning the ambulance into a mobile brothel. This scheme soon runs into difficulties.

The pair subsequently make their way to the Brittany coast. The convent nuns are amazed when Agnès, whom they believed drowned, emerges from the sea – with new novice Mona Lisa.

BOULEVARD DU RHUM 1970, France. One hundred and twenty-five minutes.

Production: SNEG (Gaumont International) *Director:* Robert Enrico *Producer:* Alain Poiré *Script:* Pierre Pelegri and Robert Enrico, from a novel by Jacques Pécheral *Photography:* Jean Boffety (Eastman Colour) *Editor:* Michel Lewin *Art director:* Max Douy *Sound:* Christian Forget *Production manager:* Paul Joly *Assistant director:* Serge Witta *Shooting:* begun on 21st September 1970; exteriors in Spain *British release details:* None *Leading players:* Brigitte Bardot (Linda Larue), Lino Ventura (Cornélius Von Zeelinga), Bill Travers (Capt Gerry Sanderson), Clive Revill (Lord Hammond), Guy Marchand (film star), Jess Hahn (Big Dutch).

Story summary: In 1920, Cornélius Von Zeelinga, rumrunner who smuggles liquor into Prohibition America, becomes rich enough to buy his own ship. At the cinema, he sees a film starring Linda Larue, and falls for her in a big way. He is determined to see all her films, and he goes from cinema to cinema from Mexico to Jamaica. He eventually meets her. For a time it seems he has made a conquest. Linda accompanies him on a cruise, but the voyage has unfortunate consequences. Cornélius loses Linda to Lord Hammond, whom she marries. Linda subsequently makes a film based on her own life. With the end of Prohibition and amnesty for the rumrunners, Cornélius is found in a cinema watching Linda's film.

LES PÉTROLEUSES (The Oil Girls) 1971, France-Spain-Italy-Great Britain. Also known as *The Legend of Frenchie King*.

Production: Francos Films (Paris); Coper Cines (Madrid); Vides Films (Rome); Hemdale Group (Great Britain) *Direction:* begun by Guy Casaril, but taken over and completed by Christian-Jaque *Producer:* Raymond Eger *Script and dialogue:* Clément Bowood, Guy Casaril and Daniel Boulanger, from an original idea by Marie-Ange Aniès and Jean Nemours *Photography:* Henri Persin (Eastman Colour) *Editor:* Nicole Gauduchon *Art director:* José-Luis Galicia *Sound:* Bernard Aubouy *Production managers:* Ignacio Gutterez and Enzo Boetani *Shooting:* begun on 18th June 1971; exteriors in Madrid and Burgos *Leading players:* Brigitte Bardot (Louise), Claudia Cardinale (Maria), Michael Pollard (Sheriff), Patty Shepard (Petite Pluie), Emma Cohen (Virginie), Teresa Cimpera (Caroline), Georges Beller (Marc), Patrick Préjean (Luc), Ricardo Salvino (Jean), Oscar Davis (Mathieu), Valery Inkijinoff (Spitting Bull), Micheline Presle (Aunt Amélie), Denise Provence (Mlle Beloiseau), Leroy Hayns (Marquis), Jacques Jouanneau (M Letellier).

Story summary: In 1880 in New Mexico, a stretch of territory is in the hands of a gang of sisters led by Louise, known as Frenchie King. When it seems there might be oil on the ranch land, Louise falls foul of Maria, who rules her four brothers with a rod of iron. The two women become rivals, though their animosity is not shared by their respective families. In fact, when the brothers and sisters are arrested, the sheriff marries the four couples before sending them for trial. Faced with this situation, Louise and Maria forget their differences, join forces and hold up the train to free their relatives before riding off together into a future of legend.

DON JUAN 1972. Announced for production, to be directed by Roger Vadim.

NOTE:

It is occasionally claimed that Brigitte Bardot's third film appearance was in *Les Dents Longues* (1952), a film directed by and featuring Daniel Gélin, whose co-star was Danièle Délorme. The contention appears to stem from an Italian-compiled list of her films; but the evidence is very slight and is not corroborated by French sources, including production information published in the trade press. A similar claim that she appeared in *Frou-Frou* (1954–55) is erroneous though having a more understandable foundation, since her name appeared fourth in the list of leading players announced when shooting began on 8th December 1954: it was only two days later that shooting started on the Bardot-starring *Futures Vedettes*.